H O

W O R K S

# Home Staging That Works

STARR C. OSBORNE

AMERICAN MANAGEMENT ASSOCIATION

New York • Atlanta • Brussels • Chicago • Mexico City
San Francisco • Shanghai • Tokyo • Toronto • Washington, D.C.

Special discounts on bulk quantities of AMACOM books are available to corporations, professional associations, and other organizations. For details, contact Special Sales Department, AMACOM, a division of American Management Association, 1601 Broadway, New York, NY 10019.
Tel: 800-250-5308    Fax: 518-891-2372
Email: specialsls@amanet.org
Website: www.amacombooks.org/go/specialsales
To view all AMACOM titles go to: www.amacombooks.org

This publication is designed to provide accurate and authoritative information in regard to the subject matter covered. It is sold with the understanding that the publisher is not engaged in rendering legal, accounting, or other professional service. If legal advice or other expert assistance is required, the services of a competent professional person should be sought.

Library of Congress Cataloging-in-Publication Data

Osborne, Starr C.
Home staging that works : sell your home in less time for more money / Starr C. Osborne.
    p. cm.
Includes bibliographical references and index.
ISBN-13: 978-0-8144-1522-1
ISBN-10: 0-8144-1522-9
1. Home staging—United States.  2. House selling—United States.  I. Title.
HD255.O82 2010
643'.12—dc22

                                                                    2009021147

Printing number
10 9 8 7 6 5 4 3 2

# C O N T E N T S

FEATURES

## A C K N O W L E D G M E N T S

This book would not be possible without the support of my agent, Kate Epstein; the gentle editing of Bob Nirkind; the enthusiasm and energy of Suzanne Lentz; the talent, vision, and humor of the indefatigable Emily Law; and the unflagging enthusiasm and perseverance of my husband, Minturn.

Have you ever told a story in front of a crowd, only to have it fall flat? Or have you ever made a suggestion you're excited about, only to meet with an awkward silence or a quick dismissal? It is a startling and uncomfortable feeling to realize suddenly that you've misjudged your audience whose outlook and taste and sense of humor are quite different from yours. When what you're putting forward is *your home*, and your audience consists of the people who are coming to look at it, and not one of them likes it enough to put in a bid—now that is a very unpleasant feeling. This book will help you avoid having that feeling when you try to sell your home. In fact, it's designed to help you sell your home quickly and for a price that makes you happy.

To make people laugh at a story or to sell them an idea, you have to know something about who they are and what they like. You don't have to know each individual in your audience, but you have to be able to sense their mood and preferences as a group. Selling your home works the same way. You won't know your potential buyers as individuals—in fact, you may not meet them at all unless they put in a bid—but you must have a feel for the group of buyers you're trying to attract. To draw buyers in, you need to create a visual story of how they could live in your home. You need to prepare your home in such a way that it "tells" them a fairy tale—in the best sense—of the wonderful life that awaits them, the life they've always wanted, in a space that not only meets their needs, but also speaks to their dreams. In short, *you need to stage your home.*

Home staging had its origins in California in the early '70s and has been booming since the early '90s, even though many people still haven't heard of it. I grew up in the '60s and '70s in New England. My childhood was one of antiques and ponies, of country lanes and moms who didn't work. Our houses were not "decorated." Fabrics were chosen to last a generation. When the fabric on a chair gave out—meaning that it split open, not that it went out of style—my mother had that one chair reupholstered. Once she had two chairs done at the same time; I remember it vividly. Threadbare chair arms reflected a worldview more than a budget.

The summer I was thirteen, my parents sent my sister and me to camp so that they could have the kitchen redone. They embarked on this renovation out of dire need, not new appliance envy. Prior to the redo, we had lived for years in a post–World War II kitchen, with lemon-colored rug squares that mom had put down and that had slowly turned brown in paths traveled most frequently by the dogs and us kids.

Houses in the right neighborhoods were bought and sold discreetly, often with handshakes. My father once bought a house over the phone, having been only in the living room for cocktails. To ask for a preinspection would have been an insult of great magnitude. Houses were often lived in for a lifetime, a backdrop to the lives lived within them.

Times have changed. Today, many buyers and sellers never meet. The buying and selling of homes have become transactions conducted at arm's length, with litigation looming behind every curtain. And the meaning of our homes has changed as well. Once upon a time, a home was primarily a shelter from the elements. Today's homes still provide shelter, but now they define us in socioeconomic ways as well. In the past ten years, the self-equals-home equation has become even stronger. What type of building we live in, what we fill it with, and how we use it reveal a lot about who we are and where we fit into our society. We judge other people by their homes and how they live in them, just as they are judging us. Does a home have overly ornate, formal curtains? A high-tech media system? A wildly disorganized home office? Immaculate tile grout? All these choices provide outside observers with clues about the people who live in that home.

Right or wrong, how we live in our homes has become a visual mission statement. Collectively, image matters—although which image we're shooting for depends on which social group we aspire to. Culturally, we are self-conscious about image and the concept of home as never before. As outward manifestations of our inner selves, our homes have become emotionally loaded in entirely new ways. Living well—however we define "well"—is now pursued by all.

This is why the shelter industry is booming in general. The mega chains have made good design and decorative arts available to all of us, and we are buying. In our homes, we're in control of our universe. We want that sense of control, to create our desired sense of self in a world grown increasingly complicated. From the safety of our homes, we feel entitled to shoot for the stars. We're buying the dream of the life that we want.

The staging industry answers these desires. At some point in the past ten years, trend spotters began to realize that if sellers could manipulate the messages their homes were sending to potential buyers, they could make more money on their home sale. Home staging started with the tactic of baking bread before open houses, and it has grown into to a full-out sensory pageant designed to excite prospective buyers' senses and fuel their dreams. Home staging has infiltrated the selling process all across the country. It's a self-feeding industry, in that every staged home raises buyers' expectations for every other home they see. A 2007 HomeGain® survey of 2,000 realtors nationwide found that 91 percent of the agents recommended that their clients have their homes staged before selling them. Clearly, staging boosts sales prices.

Most people have more of their net worth tied up in their homes than in any other single asset. Postwar bullishness and decades of skyrocketing real estate prices encouraged people to view their home as an investment.

Now, in the wake of a prolonged housing slump, many people are scrambling to realize the financial plans they made when they bought their home. If you can properly stage your home, you've greatly increased your chances not just of selling it in a tough market, but of selling it quickly and for significantly more money than you would have otherwise.

To sell your home, you must have a sense for the mood and preferences of the group of buyers you're targeting. In Chapter One, I'll show you how to figure out which group that is, but you may be wondering how it's possible for an entire group of people to share enough preferences that you could somehow make your home specifically appealing to them. The answer is that we are all products of a particular place and time in history. We're all products of the generation we grew up in. We're individuals, but we're all also members of our generational group, whether we're Baby Boomers, Gen Xers, or members of another group.

As one example of this, just look at the trends in baby names. My husband and I named our second daughter Lillie after his grandmother, whom he adored. We thought it was an uncommon and fun choice. And then I took my darling Lillie to toddler music class. Many other girls in the class were named Lillie, Lilly, or Lily. There were three in her kindergarten alone. Did we know we were naming her the equivalent of Mary in the 1950s or Karen in the 1960s? No. We thought we were being original, but we were unwitting parts of a trend. All of us are products of time and place, and anyone who thinks otherwise is seriously mistaken. So, yes, you can get a feel for the group of buyers you decide will most likely want your home, and you can stage your home to appeal directly to that group.

My company, Tailored Transitions, stages homes in Philadelphia, a city endowed with a diverse and rich architectural heritage. We stage multimillion-dollar homes, new build apartments, Louis Kahn houses abutting Fairmount Park, starter homes, and the *Philadelphia Story* altars of stone for which our city is known. (About three years ago, we actually moved clients into the house where *The Philadelphia Story* was filmed.) By walking you through the process of staging and using numerous anecdotal and visual examples of work that we've done, we are going to demystify staging.

Staging is so popular and successful that I believe it responds to some deep need. Much of staging involves simplifying a home's contents and making them more neutral; perhaps we long for these characteristics as our society grows ever more stressful, complex, and partisan. As you go through the process of staging your home, you may find that you can apply the principles of staging to other parts of your life (including your own search for a new home, but also the parts of your life unrelated to buying or selling real estate). I have found this to be so in my own life and in my clients' lives, and this aspect of staging interests me most: It can make our lives more satisfying on so many levels, beyond merely the sale of our home.

Primarily, though, this book is designed to help you tailor your home for a fast, easy, and profitable sale. I recommend that you work your way through it in an orderly manner, rather than dipping into it randomly. You may want to go back and review certain sections as you move along in the process, but basically the book is set up to guide you step by step through preparing and staging your home before you put it on the market. Here, in a nutshell, is what each chapter covers:

- ❖ Chapter One discusses what staging is, how to say good-bye to your home, why it's crucial to know who you're staging for, and how to figure out your most likely group of potential buyers.

- ❖ Chapter Two emphasizes the importance of creating a great first impression for buyers, then tells you how to improve the look of your home's exterior and entry hall to do just that.

- ❖ Chapter Three guides you through the hard work of removing your own personality from your home to make room for your prospective buyers' visions of the life they could lead in your home.

❖ Chapter Four tackles the issues of repairing and deep cleaning your home.

❖ Chapter Five guides you through the process of staging each part of your home, now that you've created more space within it and have gotten it beautifully clean and in working order. You'll learn how to bring the elements of focus, flow, color, and balance into play in staging your home to appeal directly to your most likely buyers.

❖ Chapter Six covers the nuts and bolts of getting great photographs of your property, includes a section for people who have a severely limited amount of time in which to prepare their home for sale, and provides a list of what you must do each day that your home is on the market in order to keep it ready to show.

You'll find more than forty-five features throughout the book that offer staging tips and useful information on everything from "Pruning Your Shrubs into Elegance" to "Cleaning Up After Rodents Safely" to "What About the TVs?" The book also includes sixty-five photographs, many of them before-and-after pairs, to help you better understand what good staging looks like and to illustrate points along the way. To see any of these photographs in full color—and for additional full-color photographs, information, and staging help—visit my Web site at www.tailoredtransitions.com.

Best wishes for the sale of your home, and have fun staging it!

Starr C. Osborne
President and Founder
Tailored Transitions
Philadelphia, Pennsylvania

HOME STAGING THAT WORKS

C H A P T E R

# Staging for the Right Audience

*That you may please others you must be forgetful of yourself.* —*Ovid*

**OVER THE YEARS**, you have lived in your home, designed it, furnished it, and maintained it to reflect your taste. In sum, your home is tailored perfectly for you. Unfortunately, the people who will be looking at your home during the selling process are not you. Not only are your prospective buyers likely to be younger than you, but their tastes, experiences, and expectations are guaranteed to be different from yours. And these elusive buyers are looking for their dream home. If you can transform your property into one that fits a buyer's dreams, you can sell your home. To do this, you need to figure out who your most likely buyers are and then stage your home according to what that group of people is most likely to want.

## What Is Staging?

Staging your home means transforming it to appeal to your most likely buyers. Staging is not decorating. Decorating applauds and enhances individual taste; staging removes individual taste, catering instead to the design sense and dreams of your most likely group of buyers. Changing your décor to sell your home does not mean that your existing scheme is not chic. I find myself telling some clients that their décor is too sophisticated for the market. You don't want to scare those likely buyers away. In fact, changing your décor during

*Figure 1–1. Staging brings out a home's best features and combines comfort and elegance, all without any feeling of crowding or clutter. Here, the shape of the small table's pedestal picks up the shape of the standing lamp and the colors in the throw pillows. (For a better idea of what this looks like "for real," check out my Web site.) The neutral, calm colors in the chairs and rug contrast nicely with the stark black of the stairs and the bright images on the walls.*

the staging process does not mean that it is bad in any way. All it means is that your décor is designed for you—as it should be. But you aren't buying your own home; you're trying to sell it.

In essence, staging is product packaging. You are packaging your property so that when your prospective buyers walk through it, they can envision themselves living the life they want to live, in the home they've been looking for. If you simply clean your home beautifully, perhaps tucking some of your most personal possessions out of sight, you've made a step in the right direction. However, you're nowhere near ready to put your home on the market because your home is still packaged to appeal most to *you*.

When buyers approach your home, whether via an Internet photo or in person, their analytical side may be in control. They probably have practical questions in mind. Does this home have

Figure 1–2. In real life, bathrooms are often messy, cluttered, and always personal. In a staged home, as shown in this photo, they convey a sense of sanctuary; of clean, impersonal orderliness; of having a spa right in your own home.

enough bedrooms? How many bathrooms does it have? Is it heated by gas, electric, or oil? Is it within my price range?

But buyers are also looking to fall in love with a new home. If you can appeal to your potential buyers' dreams and desires, if you can show them an idealized version of how life could be in this space, you can sell your property. With the right staging, analytical buyers can be wooed and transformed into emotional buyers. Emotional buyers want to fall in love with the home they will buy, and they will use all their analytical reasoning to support their decision. Give them the dream of how they want to live. Help your prospective buyers fall in love with your property, because if they fall in love, they'll feel they need to buy it.

## OUT WITH THE "YOU": DISENGAGING FROM YOUR HOME

The first step in staging your home is one of the hardest: taking the "you" out of your home in order to transform it into a property that speaks to the desires of your most likely buyers. Essentially, you must depersonalize your home, and, to do this, you have to be ready to say good-bye to the time you've spent there. I tell my clients that their emotional moving day is the day that staging begins. As the seller, you need to begin to emotionally disengage from your home now. To prepare yourself for the day when your property is no longer your own personal cocoon, remind yourself that your home is a product that you need to package effectively to sell for the highest price.

*Figure 1–3. Taking the "you" out of your home isn't easy, but it gets easier with practice. At some point, you may even find yourself enjoying the process!*

> ### *But My Home Goes on the Market in Just Two Weeks!*
> *If you've bought this book because you've just received the horrifying news that you have about two weeks to get your home ready for today's real estate market, you're in good hands. Of course, two weeks is not a long time. You won't be able to follow all the suggestions in this book. But read the whole book anyway, because the more you understand what good staging is and how best to reach your most likely buyers (and how to figure out who they are in the first place), the better off you'll be. In Chapter Six, the final chapter, see "If You Have Just Two Weeks to Do It All" for my advice on getting your home ready for the market when time is short. Don't follow this express route unless you have no choice. The more you do to make your home appealing to buyers, the better your chances of selling it fast.*

## SAYING GOOD-BYE TO YOUR HOME

Staging is uncomfortable. It runs contrary to the deeply held notion that our home is our castle, our refuge, the place from which we can hold the world at bay. Perhaps more significantly, staging goes against the cultural messaging that our very essence is somehow wrapped up in our homes and our possessions. In our quest to carve out a psychic space for ourselves in this world, our homes become a manifestation of who we are. If we extricate ourselves from our home, are we abandoning part of ourselves? What happens to the history we've lived through in our home? Most of all, if we depersonalize our home, aren't we taking the charm out of it? Won't it feel too cold and empty to appeal to any buyer?

Staging does nullify your taste, and that reality can be hard to accept. On the other hand, staging gives your prospective buyers what they really want: *their* taste. As uncomfortable as staging is, it is also lucrative. You'll find that it pays to stage.

Before you begin the staging process, honor your home the way it is now. This may sound silly, but a formal good-bye to your property will help you become ready to change it ruthlessly from the home you love into the home of your buyers' dreams. I often remind my clients: You are saying good-bye to your property, not what it represents.

### FIVE WAYS TO SAY GOOD-BYE

Here are five things you can do to help yourself and your family get ready to sell your home:

1. Take pictures of every room before you begin to remove the "you."

2. Throw a house cooling party, and make sure the guest list includes everyone who might be emotionally attached to the property: your immediate and extended family, your friends, your children's friends.

3. Give anyone who has possessions stored in your home a time frame in which to remove their things. If you have grown children who have left articles of their childhood in your home, give them a reasonable time to say whatever good-byes they need to say, after which they must pack up their boxes of term papers, high school trophies, favorite stuffed animals, and so on. Set a clear deadline for when their possessions must be out of the home. If they can't or won't do this themselves, pack up their childhood mementos and ship the boxes to them.

4. When you are alone in your home, turn off all phones and other electronics. Sit quietly in a room. Remember times that you have had in that room, let the space sink into you visually, noting its smell and its sounds. Don't get up until you feel you are ready to say good-bye to that room. Do the same for each room in your home.

5. Make a list of what you're going to miss most about your property: the eastern sunlight, the holly bushes, the twenty-four-hour

doorman, the Jacuzzi, whatever you've loved. Make a note of any items on the list that you want to try to find in your next property. Then make a list of what you don't like about your home—its expense, the neighborhood, the dated kitchen—and remember this list while you're looking for a new home.

Moving is stressful, even if you're happy about the reasons for your move. I have found that the emotional upheaval of leaving a home catches up with almost every client. You're better off dealing with the emotions before they blindside you, but be aware that becoming emotionally prepared to sell your home may take a while. If you have the luxury, give yourself as much time as you need. Many clients hire me and then postpone the move for six months or more. When they finally do call me, I know they're ready. When you have finished honoring your home and your time in it, you're ready for the next step: identifying your most likely buyers.

## In with the New: Figuring Out Your Target Market

A seller was about to put her four-acre, Philadelphia property on the market, and I asked who her target market was. "A blind billionaire," was her very funny reply, but she was shooting for a rather narrow target market, don't you think? You need to make your house as appealing as possible to the greatest number of prospective buyers.

Like any good marketer, before you package your product you need to have a good idea of your buyer. Just as Restoration Hardware, Gap, and Tiffany & Co. create the hang tags, boxes, and window displays for their products with a particular market in mind, so should you. First, these stores decide what type of packaging is required, and then they put their designs through rigorous test marketing and focus groups to figure out whether the product packaging encourages or discourages their various target markets to buy. Of course, you aren't going to hire a pollster to telephone 400 prospective buyers to discuss your home. You aren't going to set up neighborhood focus groups to test the market. You aren't even going to install a one-way mirror in your living room to gauge prospective buyers' reactions. In fact, there are much cheaper, easier ways to figure out who's most likely to want to buy your home. What follows is a description of the information you need and the steps you can take to get it.

### LOOKING AT THE OVERALL STATISTICS

Chances are, the person who buys your home will be younger than you. The average age for a first-time home buyer has dropped to 30, and for a repeat or move-up buyer, the average age is 47, according to a 2008 survey conducted by the National Association of Realtors. The same survey found that nearly half of all home buyers are first-time buyers. Whatever demographic you fall into, your prospective buyers are likely to fall into the generation just younger and possibly even two generations younger. The exception is when they're relocating for a job or for retirement, in which case they'll be looking for a home very similar to the one they most recently occupied. Under almost no circumstances are the new occupants of a home older than the ones moving out.

### ASKING THE PROS: INTERVIEWING REALTORS

The easiest way to further pin down your target market is to ask a realtor. Knowing who's buying properties comparable to yours is possibly the most important job of a realtor. I suggest that you set up meetings with as many as three realtors, not necessarily to hire one, but certainly to interview them. If one of them wows you, hire that one. In the meantime, glean their knowledge. Realtors you interview should come to an initial meeting with comparables; that is, properties like yours that have sold recently, who's buying them, and what they're selling for. The realtors should be able to speak intelligently about primary and secondary target markets for your home and explain how they would entice people from that target market to your home.

Typical target markets include first-time home buyers, young families, couples without children, people who are widowed or divorced, growing families, and empty nesters who are downsizing. Your realtor should be able to give you a list specific to your neighborhood and community. Ideally, he or she should understand your target market and drive that target market to your home. Once potential buyers are at your home, however, what they see there—which will be whatever you've done to prepare your home—will determine whether they decide to buy it.

---

### Questions to Ask About Probable Buyers

*Here are some questions to ask realtors and yourself about your probable buyers. You won't be able to answer them all, but just asking the questions can help you stage your property to suit potential buyers' lives:*

❖ *Are my most likely buyers married or single?*

❖ *Do they have children?*

❖ *What kinds of schools do the children attend?*

❖ *Where do my buyers tend to shop?*

❖ *How do they dress?*

❖ *Do they like to read? If so, what kinds of newspapers, magazines, and books do they favor?*

❖ *What kinds of jobs are they likely to hold?*

❖ *How do they socialize?*

❖ *What are their hobbies likely to be?*

❖ *Do they exercise? If so, how?*

---

## UNDERSTANDING THE GENERATIONS

Based on generational age, people in several demographic profiles might buy your property. From oldest to youngest, the four most probable demographic profiles for your buyers are (1) Baby Boomers, (2) Generation Jones, (3) Generation X, and (4) Generation Y. (Yes, some members of the Silent Generation and even of the Great Generation are still around, but generally, unless you are marketing a senior-living property, they are sellers, not buyers.) Defining a generation is a social science, not a hard science, and not all researchers agree on the exact profile, the time frame, or even the name for each group. Some sociologists don't even recognize Generation Jones, for example, but I feel it is a distinct and important demographic group for our purposes (perhaps because I belong to it!). What follows are general definitions of these four groups of potential home buyers, along with the characteristics specific to each.

### BABY BOOMERS

The Baby Boomers were born between 1946 and 1965, but I'm focusing on those older Boomers who were born between 1945 and 1954. Most already own homes. Their children are grown, and they are beginning to downsize. The Boomers came of age in the '60s and '70s and were largely responsible for the social revolutions of that time. Ironically, though, as they grew older they became masters of conspicuous consumption, and the sheer size of their generation meant they consumed in great quantity. They believe in a certain ease of lifestyle and have worked hard for it. Women of this generation fought bitter battles for personal and career choices that younger generations of women take for granted. In many ways, this generation believes in the American dream, either because they feel they created a new American dream with their countercultural past or because they have achieved financial success unparalleled in scope in our history.

#### *WHAT BOOMERS WANT*

When they consider buying properties, Boomers tend to look for these features:

❖ A master suite on the main living floor.

❖ His and her bathrooms and closets.

*Figure 1–4. This living room would appeal to many Baby Boomers born before 1954. The emphasis on books, the silver trophies in the bookcase, the wall sconces, and the traditional lines of the sofa mixed with the transitional-style chair all say Boomer.*

- ❖ His and her office space, ideally in separate rooms that can be closed off from the rest of the house.

- ❖ Low maintenance, especially in the yard. The wealthier ones probably own a vacation property. With multiple homes, they want to be able to just lock the door and leave.

- ❖ An eat-in kitchen, living area, and formal dining room. They like easy living but want to keep their dining room table and sideboard, with all the formal china and silver inside, even if they never use them.

❖ Great entertaining space that doesn't need a lot of upkeep.

❖ Plenty of storage for possessions that they aren't ready to part with.

❖ Ideally, new bathrooms and kitchens, but high-end materials and brand names are not as important as quality.

If your property can meet these expectations, you are going to market to Boomers.

## GENERATION JONES

The younger Baby Boomers, born between 1954 and 1965, have recently been dubbed Generation Jones. I separate them from their older generational siblings because they think differently and are looking for different things in their homes. The Generation Jones period includes 1957, when 4.3 million babies were born in the United States—the record for any year until 2007, when a preliminary estimate (released in 2008 by the National Center for Health Statistics) topped the 1957 record by about 15,000. President Barack Obama falls into Generation Jones. Unlike their older generational siblings, members of Generation Jones are still moving up in the world, or at least they like to think so. The word "Jones" in this generation's title stems from two main cultural allusions:

❖ "Keeping up with the Joneses"—an expression that arose in the populous, competitive era in which these children were born.

❖ "Jonesing"—a slang term that means "yearning" or "craving." In the optimistic '60s, Jonesers were told they could be and do and have anything. Then, as they came of age in the pessimistic '70s, they were confronted with a different reality, leaving them Jonesing for a more optimistic time—or just for more, period.

The Generation Jones kids were eating TV dinners at the kitchen table while watching the Watergate trials. Although they grew up being told they

*Figure 1–5. Jonesers like to tweak tradition. Using traditional objects, they add unexpected colors, patterns, and combinations to make things their own. They tend to have a more streamlined sensibility than their Boomer siblings.*

were Boomers, they don't remember in a truly concrete or experiential way any of the defining moments of the Boomer generation, such as the Vietnam War, the deaths of John F. Kennedy and Dr. Martin Luther King, Jr., and the Summer of Love. They were told they were defined by these events, but they were really defined by the aftermath of these events. They were on the fringe, politically and emotionally, until 2008, when they were intrinsic to the presidential election. They have become enfranchised as an age group, and they now have money. Unlike most of the Boomers, they are still raising families and moving into larger (and often higher-end) homes.

### WHAT JONESERS WANT

Jonesers look for features like these when shopping for a home:

- ❖ Plenty of bedrooms to raise their children, who are getting big.

- ❖ A separate bathroom for the children.

- ❖ Home office space, preferably not shared.

- ❖ A large family room off the kitchen for living and eating.

- ❖ A dining room if possible. This is less important to Jonesers than to Boomers, so, if pressed, they'll sacrifice it for a family room.

- ❖ Big houses. Until the Jonesers begin to downsize when their children truly leave the nest, they will want big homes; they have *arrived*.

### GENERATION X

Generation X (Gen X) followed the Jonesers. They were originally referred to as the Baby Bust Generation because of the small number of births following the post–World War II boom. Researchers differ as to which years encompass Generation X, but in his 2008 book *The Age Curve: How to Profit from the Coming Demographic Storm* (AMACOM), Kenneth Gronbach defines Gen X as the 69 million people born between 1965 and 1984. Gronbach says that this 11 percent reduction from the 78 million people born between 1945 and 1965 affects our economy and infrastructure tremendously. Gen Xers have been unfairly labeled as slackers; the truth is that there are simply fewer of them to spend money, attend schools, compete for jobs vacated by Boomers—and buy homes. Many industries that thrived under the Boomers and Jonesers have had to downsize. Think about it: The presence of fewer home buyers means a buyer's market.

Generation X buyers are 100 percent computer savvy. They read their news on the Web. They grew up in a world that bombarded them with information, and they are more likely than their generational predecessors to select only information that is of interest to them. They're usually specialists in their industry. They expect things to come easily, partly thanks to their demographic position: Because they aren't as numerous, Gen Xers have found it easier than Boomers or Jonesers to obtain a spot at a top college or in a corporate training program.

With a higher proportion of two-income households, Gen X house hunters are buying homes earlier than their predecessors. In fact, many Gen Xers become homeowners shortly after finishing their education. Research shows that Gen X buyers often get a jump start from their Boomer parents, experiencing wealth transfers long before estate and inheritance taxes are a part of the discussion. I know that I see many more parents buying high-end starter apartments for their children in this generation. This wealth transfer is becoming almost the norm in a certain upper-middle-class milieu.

These buyers do not want a fixer-upper and, because of their small number, won't have to buy one. They have been brought up to believe that image is everything and that they deserve the best. They tend to be more ironic and irreverent than the previous generation. A lengthy *Time Magazine* article (July 16, 1990) noted that the "twentysomething generation," among other things, "scornfully rejects the habits and values of the baby boomers . . . [they] grew up in a time of drugs, divorce and economic strain . . . They want flexibility . . . and a return to the sacredness of work-free weekends."

As cynical as Gen Xers sometimes seem, they still want it all—just like everyone else—but with their own definition of "all." Give it to them and you have sold your property.

### WHAT GEN XERS WANT

Here's what Gen Xers look for when shopping for a home:

* The feeling that they're keeping up with the Jonesers, but on their own terms.

* A living room and family room merged into one mega entertainment space.

* No dining room, because all of their entertaining is casual and elegant. They rarely have formal meals, because they see it as a burden to pin people down in this way. They prefer to let their guests choose what they want to eat and where they want to sit or stand.

*Figure 1–6. This Gen X room is spare and lean. Its focus is on the wooden floors and the windows, not on the objects. The one piece of furniture with traditional lines—the armchair—has a huge oversized fabric on it, conveying the Gen X tendency toward irreverence. The framed advertising posters and sisal rugs also speak to this generation.*

❖ Green homes, because they are worried about the climate.

❖ Simple, sleek lines, because they disdain pomp.

❖ Modern styling. Think iconic furniture at the Museum of Modern Art. Gen Xers favor quirky little collections of kitsch and large color-field paintings.

❖ Bureaus tucked away in walk-in closets, because Gen Xers place importance on screening out stress.

❖ Homes wired for music, TV, and the Internet.

❖ Abundant counter space in the kitchen.

❖ Lots of storage and closet space, behind closed doors—no open storage for this generation.

❖ A large yard to play in with their children and animals and in which to connect with the earth.

### GENERATION Y

Generation Y—also called Echo Boomers or Millennials—initially peaked in 1990 with nearly 4.2 million births in that year alone. After that the birthrate dipped mildly, then began to rise steadily toward the record year of 2007. Some demographers think Gen Y ended around the year 2000, but Gronbach, for example, projects that this generation will end in 2010, ultimately reaching a total of 100 million members.

Members of Gen Y have been marketed to ever since their parents played Mozart for them as babies. They expect everything that is promised to them on the Web sites they frequent and in the catalogs that flood their mailboxes. From cars to carpets to carrots, everything is painstakingly packaged to capture their fancy, and it has been for as long as they can remember. Generation Y is still defining itself, and its members are just beginning to be a market force. Already, though, they're beginning to flood the housing market, purchasing homes even earlier than their older siblings. Keep your eye on them: They will be buyers to pursue in the next few years.

### WHAT GEN YERS WANT

These features appeal to Gen Yers as they look to buy homes:

❖ Wired properties—fireplaces and curtains should all work on the same clicker.

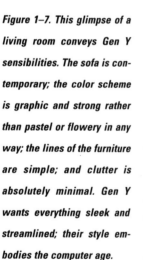

*Figure 1–7. This glimpse of a living room conveys Gen Y sensibilities. The sofa is contemporary; the color scheme is graphic and strong rather than pastel or flowery in any way; the lines of the furniture are simple; and clutter is absolutely minimal. Gen Y wants everything sleek and streamlined; their style embodies the computer age.*

❖ Ease, such as wood-burning fireplaces that are ideally con-
verted to gas.

❖ Bathrooms that are spas.

❖ Abundant office space (at least one workroom per person),
because work and home life have been blurred. Gen Yers live
their jobs, or else they would not do them. Many will sacrifice a
bedroom or two for good office space.

❖ High-end luxury items, which they believe they deserve and for
which they'll forsake some of the basics. They might buy a state-
of-the-art sound system before buying a dinner table.

## MEDIA INFLUENCE ON THE GENERATIONS

The younger we are, the more influence the media has had over our generation. The Baby Boomers remember when there was no TV, and even many
Jonesers remember not having a TV when they were young. The Gen Xers
grew up on the computer. Generation Y members do not remember a time
without the Internet.

Retailers have spent untold dollars on market research to manipulate
our dreams and desires. In the media, advertisers continue to emphasize the
importance of lifestyle to sell product. One of the inadvertent results of this
media saturation is that many buyers today want their homes to be both
completely wired and their retreat from the world, their private escape from
the constant barrage from the wired world. With further irony, how that
oasis looks is completely defined by the media. Many buyers don't want
bathrooms, but prefer a home spa. They don't want a bedroom, they want an
escape from the world with 400-thread-count hotel sheets that they saw in a
magazine or on TV. In sum, although today's buyers are more visually
sophisticated than any generation in history, they are increasingly culturally
homogeneous. Because they come by their taste from mass culture, their
taste is defined by mass culture.

### DECIDING ON YOUR TARGET GENERATION

Ultimately, your ability to target your generational buyers and capture their imagination will sell your property. You needn't get rid of your furnishings or buy all new upholstery from a store where your buyers are likely to shop. I am recommending that you give your potential buyers the visual clues (as defined by the media and by your buyers' generation) that your house is worthy of them. (And, of course, some aspects of staging—like creating space, cleaning, and making repairs [see Chapters Two through Four]—transcend generational differences.)

So think about who these buyers are and who are most likely to buy your home. We all know them. We work with them. Some of them are relatives. If you can infuse your home with these buyers' dreams, you can sell it. Properties sell when they speak to their target market. Pick the profile of your most likely buyers and focus on that demographic.

## DETERMINING YOUR MARKET BY THE TIME YOU'VE SPENT IN YOUR HOME

If you're still confused about who your target market is, try this formula:

* If you've been in your home five years or less, your own cultural generation is your target market.

* If you've been in your home fewer than fifteen years, the next generation younger is your target market.

* If you've been in your home more than fifteen years, jump two generations younger.

If you start using this formula on yourself and on your friends and family, you'll quickly see that the great majority of homes should be staged to appeal to Generation Jones or Gen X. Think of someone in this age group who seems to have the means to purchase your property. Ideally, the buyer should not be someone you know particularly well. Put this person's face on the image of your buyer. Keep thinking of this person, as well as how much he or she differs from you, as you read the following chapters. This imagery will help you keep your taste out of the staging process as you insert your statistically probable buyers' taste into your home.

## THE NEXT STEP: CREATING A GREAT FIRST IMPRESSION

Now that you've identified your most likely target market, you're ready to start transforming your home into a place that will appeal tremendously to that market. The first thing buyers will see is the entrance to your home, whether they see it online or in person. In the next chapter, you'll learn how to wow your buyers in that first crucial viewing.

# First Impressions

*All the world's a stage, and all the men and women merely players; they have their exits and their entrances. . .* —*Shakespeare*, As You Like It

**DO YOU REMEMBER** how you felt when you first saw the home you eventually bought? To sell it, you must arouse those same feelings in prospective buyers. Nobody must buy your property—and nobody will—unless they fall in love with it. The process of falling in love must begin the minute prospective buyers see your home. Your goal is to make sure that nothing interrupts or derails your buyers' delight as they walk through your home.

A few years ago I staged a wonderful turn-of-the-century farmhouse on seven acres of land. The property was a Currier & Ives dream, approached through a long allée of linden trees. In front of the home, a towering oak graced an island in the middle of a roundabout. The entry was impressive: a double-sized front door opened into a stone anteroom, which led into a magnificent hall with soaring ceilings, a dramatic federal staircase, and a view to an oversized living room and library. Enchanted by these sights, I lingered in the hall to take them in. Then my eyes wandered downward . . . to the stained, peeling, faux marble vinyl flooring. And I suddenly felt less enchanted.

First impressions count. Buyers may approach your home with a mental checklist that includes basic needs: price, value, location, and schools, as well as other factors tabulated by the logical part of their brain. However, all these practical considerations may fly out the window in the face of a more immediate and instantaneous emotional response.

*Figure 2–1.* **Before:** *Although this living room may be cozy in real life, the photograph overemphasizes its contents, making the room appear small and cluttered.*

In his best-selling book *Blink: The Power of Thinking without Thinking*, author Malcolm Gladwell makes the case that the majority of our decisions are formed in just a fraction of a second. We take in a huge amount of information each day—more than our colonial ancestors did in a lifetime. To survive, we sort and stockpile what our minds take in, performing a kind of instantaneous quality control. Whenever we're confronted with new information, we automatically sift through the data we've already stored, an action Gladwell calls thin slicing, to form an instant impression.

Based on their instantaneous impression of your home, buyers will make assumptions about the rest of your property that may or may not be true. If your yard is beautiful and well maintained, they assume the whole

*Figure 2–2.* **After:** *Removing books and lamps helps unclutter the look of the living room, as does repositioning the furniture. Now the photograph highlights the space and not the objects, so that the room appears large and inviting.*

house has been kept up. If, on the other hand, your yard is filled with weeds, they assume the rest of the property has also been neglected. If the lobby in your building has trash on the floor, buyers may feel prejudiced against your condo even before they step over your threshold. By paying close attention to what your buyers see in these first critical moments, you will ensure that any of their emotional leaps will be in your favor.

In this chapter, you'll learn how to use the power of split-second decision making to your best advantage when selling your home. Using the knowledge gained in Chapter One about the profile of your target buyer, you'll learn how to stage your home to create a favorable first impression. Whether you have a row home, a split-level condo, or a Victorian bungalow, these tools and techniques are designed to put your home in its best light from the moment buyers first see it.

## THE FIRST LOOK: ATTRACTING INTERNET SHOPPERS

These days, your prospective buyers are probably forming their first impression of your home while cruising the Internet. About 90 percent of today's home buyers look at real estate listings on the Web before shopping by car or on foot. Even if buyers aren't scanning the listings themselves, their realtors will do it for them, e-mailing customers those that suit their needs—most with photos attached. I promise you that a less-than-perfect presentation of your photos will turn off potential buyers, especially when you're trying to attract those coveted relocation buyers with limited real-time viewing opportunities. These are the buyers you most want to attract—the ones with a relocation budget and a time crunch.

Good photographs make the most of what you have: accentuating the positive features of your home and minimizing any negatives. Use every picture slot on the listing. If you don't have enough rooms, fill in with mood-setting close-ups. In Chapter Six, I'll explain the nuts and bolts of taking flattering photographs that draw buyers in.

## THE DRIVE-BY: MAKING THE MOST OF A BUYER'S SECOND LOOK

The drive-by gives buyers the opportunity to preview a handful of properties in person. If you've managed to lure buyers off the Internet and onto your street, this is your chance to build on a strong first impression. You want to make the most of this opportunity so that buyers will remember your property in a good way.

Perhaps you've been told that your property lacks curb appeal. Loosely translated, this phase means that your home doesn't make a good first impression from the street. Until about ten years ago, realtors would mention curb appeal as something a home either did or didn't have, as opposed to something to strive for. In fact, any home—even ones with no natural curb appeal—can be made to look better. Home staging begins out front! (In later chapters, you'll learn how to stage the rest of your home and any outbuildings.)

### STAGING THE EXTERIOR

The first rule of exterior home staging is to make your property appear easy to maintain. If you live in a neighborhood with sidewalks, you may capture foot traffic from those in nearby neighborhoods looking to move up. These buyers have a close view, so you will have to take extra pains with outdoor maintenance. Make sure the sidewalk in front of your home is clear of leaves, weeds, branches, and litter. For a clean look, edge with a weed trimmer or shears. Depending on the season, keep your sidewalk weeded, swept, leaf-free, shoveled, and possibly salted. Keep any grass along the sidewalk trimmed or raked. Remove all icicles from the roof—a sign to buyers of neglect, poor insulation, or both. Straighten the for-sale sign; a crooked one makes the whole property look shabby.

If you're selling an apartment, condo, or co-op, you may have to keep after your landlord to tidy up walks and flower beds. Make sure your lobby is neat and clean; you may get a few interested buyers poking around inside before they even contact you or your realtor. I've known sellers to wash the front door of their building, clean glass doors or windows in the lobby, or clean the walls of their elevator; they do whatever it takes to make a great initial impression.

This goes for closely settled neighborhoods too. Perhaps you're trying to sell your rowhouse, duplex, twin, or townhouse, or maybe your adjoining neighbors' yards run extremely close to your house. If their properties look cluttered and unkempt, they bring down the appeal of yours. Asking neighbors for permission to tidy up *their* property a bit along with your own calls for tricky diplomacy. Either their property is a mess because they think it's fine that way, or they're in financial straits or some other difficulty and may be embarrassed about their property but just can't tackle it at the moment. Either way, this isn't the time to nickel-and-dime your neighbors by asking them to pay you back for work done. Instead, try telling them that your realtor is driving you nuts, hounding you to get the whole area looking consistent. Tell them you would be so grateful if they would allow you to mow their front lawns (with your mower, not theirs), perhaps

**Figure 2–3.** Before: *The entrance area to this home is too cluttered with the family's personal items—including a bag of road salt, which reminds buyers of work. The artsy benches are quirky, and they crowd what is a large door.*

*Figure 2–4.* **After:** *Even in early spring, before the flower beds are in full sway, this entrance area is improved by removing the clutter that crowded the door, by installing a large, new doormat, by placing a few attractive planters with flowers, by trimming back the vines around the door area, and by putting some plants into the gardens that flank the stairs. By cleaning up and giving the door some space, the area seems larger and more gracious. See also Figures 2–7 and 2–8.*

weed or shovel their sidewalks along with your own, maybe even throw some extra mulch down for them when you do your own front garden, in addition to keeping an eye out for litter and debris—*just* while you're trying to sell your home, even though you think the realtor is being ridiculous about this. Would they mind? Of course, you wouldn't charge them for letting you intrude like this. This approach may work. Try it.

> ### *Be Up-Front About Problems*
>
> *Staging isn't about covering up existing issues. If you're aware of a problem in your home, don't try to cover it up. Offering full disclosure reassures buyers that you're not trying to trick them and that everything else in your home is in good repair. Putting a price on the problem—for example, obtaining a professional estimate for a new roof—stops buyers from worrying about the scope of the repair.*

### THE APPROACH: DRIVEWAYS AND WALKS

Last summer, I was asked to give an estimate for staging a $2 million house. With high expectations, I swung my car into the client's road. Just as my GPS informed me that I had arrived at my destination, I spotted the street number on an odd-looking mailbox. But what was this? Closer inspection revealed that the mailbox was shaped like a fat, pink cow with horns and a dangling udder. I rechecked my address, but this was indeed the entrance to the $2 million property. The home itself was hidden down a long driveway. Greeting visitors with your own brand of kitsch or humor in this way is completely fine, except when your visitors are prospective buyers.

This advice applies to yard sculpture and signs as well. Starting from the street, head toward your own front door and notice what you see on the way. Is your mailbox one that people comment on (using words like "cute" or "interesting" or "unusual")? If so, replace it with a more conservative one. Do you have a wooden pig or some other creature visible in your yard? Maybe some stone bunnies or a plastic windmill? A nonfunctioning birdhouse? A blow-up jack-o-lantern or Santa, depending on the season? Anything (like a sign or sculpture) that reveals your political or religious leaning? Any items that your neighbors have actually joked or complained about? Remove all such examples of your personal taste. Using the oh-isn't-that-cute/interesting/unusual? test in your mind can help you decide what should go. Remember, anything you remove now can grace your next home if you so choose.

All driveways should be invisible. Few of them are beautiful. (How many of us have a sweeping drive flanked by towering maples?) Since there isn't much you can do to beautify the appearance of your driveway, at least try to make it look as pristine as possible.

Begin by having your driveway power-washed, and if it's more than five years old, have it resealed. The cost is negligible and well worth it when you consider the vast improvement in appearance resealing will make. If you have a gravel driveway, get it freshly resurfaced. Buyers shouldn't see any bare dirt or weeds poking out from beneath the crushed rock. Finally, give your driveway a haircut by trimming any encroaching grass. Keep your driveway free of leaves in the fall, and shoveled or plowed in the winter.

For walkways, remove weeds, leaves, snow, and ice as needed. Make sure your prospective buyers won't be stumbling over any loose bricks, stones, or uneven pieces of concrete (see also Chapter Four for suggestions about what repairs or changes to make). If any shrubs are looming over or into your walkways, prune them back (in a graceful way, not butchering them! See "Pruning Your Shrubs into Elegance") so that buyers don't have to beat them off as they try to reach your door.

Enhancing your driveway or walk with soft lighting is also a good idea. Many drive-by viewings take place at night (the only time many buyers are available), and solar-powered lights, even from a distance, add drama and impact to your home. This quick fix is relatively inexpensive; solar-powered lights can be purchased at any large home supply store.

**THE FRONT YARD**

Staging a yard isn't complicated; what you have to do is make the yard look easy to maintain. Pruning, weeding, mulching, edging, and mowing are your best friends in successful yard staging: *prune* the bushes, *weed* everything, *mulch* and *edge* the beds, and *mow* all the grass. Do these tasks and your property will appear low maintenance, whether or not it actually is.

When mulching around trees or shrubs, be sure to keep the mulch clear of the trunks. A common mistake is to pile the mulch right up around the trunk. This just makes the trunk more susceptible to damp and disease and helps to suffocate your plantings.

If you have garden beds, mulch them with black mushroom mulch. Never use that red stuff! Not only does it clash with most homes and plants, drawing the worst kind of attention to itself, but also it's a big favorite in flower beds at gas stations and fast food chains. Enough said.

### Pruning Your Shrubs into Elegance

*Skillful pruning can do wonders for any shrub. "Skillful" does not mean giving your shrubs a buzz cut or making them into perfect geometric shapes with an electric hedge trimmer. (This is what I meant when I said not to butcher overgrown shrubs.) Pruning—with good pruning tools—should remove branches that are dead, that are growing in a way that isn't constructive or flattering to the plant, or that are just way too long. Good pruning enhances a shrub's natural form rather than shaving or hacking it into a totally unnatural form. If you aren't an experienced pruner and can't afford to hire one, buy or borrow a book on pruning and see if you can bring new life and elegance to your shrubs yourself.*

If a shrub is way too big for its spot or too far gone for help, dig it out. Even if you don't have the budget to buy new shrubs and other plantings for your yard (and many homeowners don't), you can fill in the new gaps with mulch, crushed rock or interesting large stones, or some inexpensive annual flowers, depending on the season. Yews that have been growing unchecked for years rarely look good, and many homes feature at least one of these. If a yew or other shrub is blocking a window, covering too much of your home's front, or just generally giving your home a funereal look, you should probably remove it.

If your budget allows you to buy new plants, follow the tough love rule: Use shrubs that are deer resistant, kid resistant, pet resistant, low maintenance, and not shocked when planted (meaning that they don't take months to adjust to their new soil, looking horrible in the meantime).

*Figure 2–5.* **Before:** *As they approach this door, buyers will brace themselves for a morass of student clutter inside. Certainly, the entrance area doesn't appear cared for or particularly welcoming.*

*Figure 2–6.* **After:** *With an enormous new doormat; a neatly hung apartment number; a balanced, welcoming splash of color on either side; and personal clutter removed, this entrance area still conforms to the building's rules, yet it is much more inviting.*

If you live in an apartment, condo, or co-op, containers and pots of flowers provide a splash of color for little cost. In the summer, pots of petunias, geraniums, or lovely blue lobelia, combined with dusty miller and marigolds, can cheer up any entrance. Brightly colored chrysanthemums in a wooden crate or planter are lovely in the fall. In the winter months, set out a basket or container with rich, green magnolia leaves adorned by red twig dogwood. In early spring, a basket of

planted pansies that have been hardened off (that is, gradually introduced to the cold outdoor air) is a welcoming sight at your front door.

### Five Good Shrubs for Staged Yards

*Here are some bushes that pass the hardiness test, look good year-round, pack a visual punch, and are more interesting than just another yew. Check with a local garden center to find out which ones grow best in your area (or to get other recommendations).*

❖ *Dwarf cherry laurel. This compact evergreen shrub is perfect for gardening-challenged homeowners. It can grow in full shade to partial sun, making it a candidate for tough foundation areas. It has abundant small white flowers in late spring and doesn't go into shock after planting. It's even deer resistant. What more could you want?*

❖ *Holly. These are my favorite shrubs to plant in the winter. They are evergreen, festive, and hopeful, with their red berries and waxy leaves. Holly needs full to partial sun and can be grown in just about any part of the country. See what your local garden center has in stock. The female plants have bright berries. Hollies are common enough that someone nearby probably owns a male plant that will propagate the female plant you buy.*

❖ *Nandina, or heavenly bamboo. This heavenly evergreen is not really bamboo and thank goodness, because real bamboo is relentlessly invasive. Avoid real bamboo, but nandina is lovely. It bears red berries in winter, blooms with white flowers in spring, and displays spectacular red foliage in fall. See which varieties are available in your area, and create instant splendor in your yard.*

❖ *Viburnum. With over 150 species of viburnum available, you can find a variety to suit any need: wet or dry, sun or shade, natural or formal, shrub or tree, native or exotic, deciduous or evergreen. Make sure you're buying the type you want! Bloom times span early spring through June and are followed by attractive fruit and outstanding fall foliage.*

> ❖ *Hydrangea. Hydrangeas aren't evergreen, but they make up for this flaw with their beautiful, long-lasting blooms, with their tolerance for everything from full sun to nearly full shade, and with their graceful form even in the winter, especially if you leave their flower heads on.*

### CREATING A STAGED GARDEN

Many homes today have gardens; maybe a patch of color and beauty in the front yard and maybe a more elaborate flower or vegetable garden out back. Regardless of where your garden is located, you want it to appear the same as the yard if possible: low maintenance. Sure, you may get prospective buyers who adore gardening and fall in love with your perennial bed. If your flower beds are garden tour material, keep them as they are even if they're a lot of work; for the right buyer they'll be a selling point, and undoing your gardens will be more trouble (and heartache) than it's worth. But do realize that buyers who have never touched a trowel in their lives may look at your carefully tended English garden and just see a giant headache.

On the other hand, if your garden is the Cancún of the weed world, where weeds go to relax and renew themselves, you should rip it all out and put in something relatively easy to plan, plant, and maintain during the selling process. Create a garden that is disciplined, with plants layered by height for an architectural effect. Start in the back with a row of bushes, followed by a middle row of medium to tall flowers, and in front a hardy ground cover. Think of it as you would a flower arrangement, not a growing and evolving garden, but one that will look good just long enough to sell your home.

At the homes I stage, we keep gardens looking their best by putting in new specimens every couple of weeks. If you're doing your own staging, your best bet economically is to rely on hardy plants that are good performers, ones that you can count on to remain in bloom for some time.

### Fifteen Plants for Varying Sun Conditions

*Again, keeping in mind that you should check with your local garden center to find out which plants are best for your soil and sun conditions, here are some of my favorite plants for full sun:*

*Echinacea, or coneflower. This hardy perennial (usually pink with large dark centers, occasionally white) blooms from July to September.*

*Lamb's ears. A great border plant with silvery fuzzy leaves, lamb's ears produce light purple flowers on tall spikes. The flower spikes reach 12 to 18 inches in height, but the rest of the plant stays much closer to the ground.*

*Marigold. A prolific small bloomer through the fall, this annual adds energy and warm yellows, oranges, and reds to the garden.*

*Chrysanthemum. This annual has brushlike flowers and provides many blooms in the fall. Stay away from the garish colors; white, yellow, and rust are best. Be warned: Many white chrysanthemums become tinged with a sickly lavender hue before the season ends.*

*Sedum. A perennial with great foliage that looks almost succulent, this plant is also popular because it grows well in poor soil, has leaves that change color in the fall, and produces tiny clusters of pink flowers that last, last, last.*

*Geranium. This common annual is always a crowd pleaser and holds up incredibly well with minimal care; it needs just periodic watering and deadheading (i.e., removing flower heads that are past their prime). Its perennial cousin, the cranesbill, also has a long blooming season and a showy appearance.*

*Portulaca. This annual ground cover blooms in the late spring through fall and does well in hot, dry climates. Homeowners love it for its ease of maintenance; no deadheading is required. It's one of my favorite performers.*

**Snapdragon.** *This annual creates colorful flower spikes that open gradually, from the bottom to the top. Snapdragons are available in two heights: Dwarf varieties grow to about 10 inches, and the taller types grow to a height of 18 to 24 inches. A single snapdragon plant may produce seven or eight blossom spikes in the course of a summer.*

**Shasta Daisy.** *This hardy plant grows all over the United States and creates bushy plants with many white flowers and yellow eyes. With its hardiness, simplicity, and beauty, it works well in any garden.*

### Here Are My Top-Performing Plants for Shade

**Vinca.** *This dark evergreen is an ideal ground cover for shady spots, with sparse blue-purple flowers in spring. Use it instead of ivy or pachysandra.*

**Kale.** *This is my hands-down fall and winter garden winner. The attractive lettucelike leaves of this annual grow more vibrant in color as the weather gets colder. Colors range in shades of pink, rose, magenta, and white to creamy yellow. The outer leaves are often in shades of blue-gray-green to bronze.*

**Phlox.** *This great perennial comes in many varieties and colors. All of them bloom for weeks and weeks and provide great value in the garden.*

**Coralbell.** *This plant begins blooming in early June and doesn't stop until the end of August, but, even more than their tiny flowers, I love their foliage. I suggest deadheading to prolong the blooming season.*

**Pansy.** *This annual comes in all colors and is a great early spring bloomer that works in shade or sun. A new hardy variety creates a wonderful splash of color in both fall and winter.*

**Coleus.** *A showy annual planted for its many colored leaves, this plant lights up shady corners, grows fast, and transplants easily to new locations.*

## THE FAÇADE: LOOKING GOOD

Some homes are beautiful on the outside. Those that make the strongest first impression tend to be all-brick houses, houses trimmed in brick or stone, or sided in wood (planks, shingles, or logs). If your home is one of these, count your blessings. If it isn't, there's still a lot you can do to spiff up its appearance.

First, power-wash the outside of your home until it sparkles. Wash all the windows so that, even from the outside, they look good. If your house hasn't been painted in the last five years, consider investing in a fresh coat. Even if the paint isn't cracking and peeling, a new paint job assures buyers that this is one less thing they'll have to spend money on.

If you decide to repaint, choose a color that flatters your home, adds to its curb appeal, and isn't quirky. Steer clear of cool colors like mint or sage green that clash with or fade into the landscape. Forget about pastel blue, pastel pink, or lavender anything. Instead, go for neutral hues. Cream or tan are warm colors and look good on almost any style of home. (If you know you're color challenged or your tastes tend toward the unusual, get advice on colors from a realtor or a friend you've always considered very conservative, maybe even a little dull.) I tend to prefer Benjamin Moore paint, and the color names and numbers I've listed in this chapter refer to Benjamin Moore choices. But you can get any color indicated here matched to another brand.

Now look at your roof. When it comes to first impressions, a roof can be a real hot button. In addition to creating a poor impression, a shabby roof signals the need for high repair or replacement costs to savvy buyers. If you don't have the budget for repairs, get an estimate from a respected roofing firm for the repair or replacement cost, and disclose this to your sellers. Buyers will appreciate your honesty and assume everything else in your home is in good shape. (This also holds true for other major repairs.)

If you have a problem that's fixable—a tree branch hanging over a corner of the roof, a missing shingle—take the time to make the repair. It's well worth the expense. You should also have your gutters cleaned and make sure your downspouts are in place. Pools of standing water around your property are a red flag for buyers and could derail an otherwise delightful first impression.

> ### *Best Choices for Exterior Paint Colors*
> *Here are some of my favorite exterior home colors:*
>
> ❖ *Mascarpone Cream (AF–20)*
>
> ❖ *Windham Cream (HC–6)*
>
> ❖ *Jute (AF–80)*
>
> ❖ *Weston Flax (HC–5)*
>
> ❖ *Wilmington Tan (HC–34)*
>
> *Good colors for exterior shutters include:*
>
> ❖ *Wenge (AF–180)—a dark color that's not quite black*
>
> ❖ *Hale Navy (HC–154)*
>
> ❖ *Flint (AF–560)—medium gray*

## THE FRONT DOOR

It's amazing how many home sales end at the front door. To you, your front door is just an entry. For buyers, it's a metaphor; a beautiful front door says care and quality, whereas one in disrepair is an immediate red flag. If you're on a limited budget, begin your staging effort here.

Many front doors with potential are hiding their beauty behind metal or plastic screen doors. If you have a cheap screen door, remove it. You will be amazed at how your entry is transformed. It's better to have no screen door than a cheesy one.

If your front door is old and shabby, replace it with a new wooden one. Choose one with windows, either on top or all the way down. If you have a dark entry hall, glass isn't an option; it's a necessity. If you already have a door with

*Figure 2–7.* **Before:** *This dirty front door appears neglected. The house numbers are "ye olde" black wrought iron style that was popular from post–World War II through the 1970s. Notice the damage that some poorly behaved dog has done to the lower left door frame.*

*Figure 2–8.* **After:** *After cleaning and repainting the door and its surrounding area, replacing "ye olde" numbers with new brass ones, the front door now seems worthy of a quality home.*

a window, remove any curtains, shades, or privacy screens. While your home is on the market, your goal is let buyers see inside and to let light pour into your entry.

At the very least, make sure your front door is clean. Cleaning makes an immediate improvement. Power-wash or scrub the surface, removing any dirt or cobwebs. If there are

sidelights, clean them until they sparkle inside and out. Weather-stripping on your door should be replaced if it's ragged or worn.

Repainting your front door is also a good investment. Trust me, your door needs a fresh coat! When choosing a color, be sure to pick one that complements your exterior (and interior) color scheme. Red, black, midnight blue, and dark green are good color choices for front doors.

### Welcoming Front Door Colors

*These colors will help draw prospective buyers into your home:*

❖ *Meditation (AF–395)—high-gloss tan, great for a brick house; contains just enough green to be pretty without creating a Christmas tree effect*

❖ *Schooner (AF–520)—an elegant French blue*

❖ *Van Deusen Blue (HC–155)—a grayer cousin to Schooner; also elegant*

❖ *Red Parrot (1308) or Caliente (AF–290)—good classy reds for the front door to warm up a gray or stucco home*

❖ *Absolute Green (2042–10)—rich, almost black green; looks great in high gloss*

❖ *Green Bay (2045–10)—greener than Absolute Green and another of my favorites*

Painting your front door gives you an opportunity to add a little pizzazz to the exterior of your home. And if you're going to paint your front door, you may as well take the time to polish the hardware, or—if it's old or insubstantial—replace it. The doorknob is the first thing prospective buyers will touch, and you want yours to feel like a top-of-the-line product. The same holds true for your lock; if it's a cheap one, replace it with something better, like a Medeco. Locks are status symbols that tell buyers you have a home worth protecting.

*Figure 2–9.* **Before:** *This front door has promise. The stone of the house makes a lovely background, the porch architecture is charming, and the path has a somewhat "secret garden" feeling. But it's eclipsed by clutter: two doormats, wind chimes, overgrown bushes, empty planters, lanterns hung askew, a yellow sign, and other distracting visual information.*

If you live in a condo or apartment, you may be unable to replace your ugly metal door, or one that is standard in your building. Find out if you can at least repaint your door or change the locks or hardware. A shiny new brass door knocker makes a welcoming impression.

### OTHER OUTSIDE ENTRY IDEAS

Your door isn't the only thing buyers will notice while standing at your entry. Whether you own a home, condo, or co-op, if you have a brightly colored,

*Figure 2–10.* **After: With the clutter gone and the large, overgrown shrub removed, the front door is now visible and gives buyers the impression of a well-maintained house before they step inside.**

attention-seeking front doormat or one made of plastic, replace it with a large, neutral sisal mat. Steer clear of cute doormats with messages or pictures; you're going for a look that says quality. Choose an oversized mat. The larger the mat, the larger your doorway will seem.

Showcase your lighting fixture as well. Many showings take place at night, and the last thing you want is for buyers standing on your front porch to notice a cracked globe, a burned-out bulb, or a cluster of cobwebs. If your porch fixture is in good shape, remove the glass and wash it thoroughly. If it's old or doesn't complement the home, consider replacing it with a more flattering one. All these small touches may seem insignificant, but they are things your buyers will notice while standing at your entry, waiting to come inside.

*Figure 2–11.* **Before:** *Looking from the front hall into the living room, the layout of furniture blocks prospective buyers' view of the winterized porch beyond. Visitors are visually waylaid by all the objects between them and the porch.*

*Figure 2–12.* After: *A more streamlined layout pulls prospective buyers into the living room and to the porch beyond. Now they can easily absorb the architecture without being bothered by the owner's many objects.*

## The Inside Entry: Creating a Sense of Welcome

In the home staging business, we advise our clients to stage their entry foyer or hall to create a welcoming first impression. This isn't about putting out trays of cookies (something we don't recommend). Nor is it about creating a serene space, although buyers do tend to feel more comfortable in a tranquil setting. In stager's terms, a welcoming space is one that *invites you in* and *lures you into the rest of the house.* Stagers create welcoming spaces by appealing to buyers' emotions.

Perhaps you have come to think of your front hall or foyer as a throw-away space, and that may be fine—but not when you're selling. In a welcoming home, the entry is an *entrée* that sets up expectations of the main course to come. Here is where buyers anticipate the rest of the house. For those of you in an apartment, condo, or co-op, the front hall presents the first opportunity for your home to be judged.

Your entry should also allow buyers to move in psychologically. You want them to be able to picture themselves in the home, so you need to remove as much of your clutter and personal effects as possible.

> ### *Scent or Stench?*
> *Many sellers and overzealous stagers keep scented candles lit in the entry hall or bathroom, or they spray air freshener throughout the home. Please don't do this. People have strong reactions to smells, and some scents aggravate allergies. Worse, buyers may suspect that you are try-ing to mask an unpleasant odor.*

To see whether your entry says "Welcome!" to prospective buyers, try this test. Take a yardstick and tape it to the base of the door so that it extends the swing of the door. With the door in any position, the yardstick should hit walls, not furniture. If any furniture falls within the arc, it's blocking the sense of welcome in the room and should be removed. If you can extend the arc that the door makes by 30 inches, great. Eighteen inches of free space beyond the actual swing of the door is an absolute minimum.

Next, examine your sightlines. Both visually and physically, buyers should be able to move easily from your front hall into the rooms beyond (see Figures 2–11 and 2–12). If any chairs or sofas block your path or have their backs to you, consider moving them to another location. You don't want your couch to function as an upholstered sawhorse, physically and mentally blocking access to the entrance of a room. Ideally, every sightline from this vantage point should lure you farther into the home.

Although all entries are not created equal—they come in a variety of shapes and sizes and lead to different spaces beyond—I can give you general rules for staging them to best effect. Even if your home has no actual entry hall or vestibule and your front door opens directly into a main room, you can create a good first impression. Simply take the following steps (ignore the first one if you have no hall closet, of course).

### BEGIN WITH YOUR HALL CLOSET

A cluttered hall closet is a signal to buyers that you're short on space. Remove less frequently used or off-season coats or jackets, and do the same with any shoes or boots. Make sure any items on closet shelves are neatly stored and stacked. Replace the motley assortment of hangers with pretty wooden ones (about $10 for a set of five at most hardware stores). Uniform wooden hangers make even small closets look presentable. Go a step further for a neat appearance and organize your coats according to length and color. As a rule, while your home is on the market, your hall closet should be no more than half full. If you have open hooks rather than a closet, don't think that you are off the proverbial hook. Minimizing is even more important in this case, so leave as few coats hanging as you possibly can.

### PROVIDE SEATING IF POSSIBLE

If—and only if—you can do so without crowding the front door (see the tip on using a yardstick), furnish your entry area with a comfortable chair or bench where visitors can sit to remove outerwear, and provide a place (such as a mat or shoe rack) to store their muddy shoes or boots. You don't want them to linger; you do want them to feel at home.

### UNCLUTTER THE SPACE

Clutter is distracting to buyers, pulling their focus away from the house itself and stopping them in their tracks. Remove any large pieces of furniture that block entrance into the surrounding space, and pack away the smaller things that tend to clutter hallway surfaces (such as keys, cell phones, your spouse's watch, unread mail) and floors (shoes, boots, umbrellas, bike pumps). Pack up any items of a personal or possibly contentious nature, just as you did outside (see also Chapter Three).

*Figure 2–13.* **Before: This front hall is cluttered with family items—a signal to buyers that the closet is too small for today's active family.**

## MAKE USE OF MIRRORS

Small pictures on the walls tend to distract buyers and keep them from moving on. Instead, hang one large mirror to achieve a sense of space and light, or hang two mirrors across from one another to add dimension to the room. Mirrors work magic: Buyers who see themselves in a mirror may subconsciously insert themselves into the space.

*Figure 2–14.* **After: Removing the family's personal items allows the buyer to enter the space both physically and psychologically. The new rug gives the hall its own character without making it feel cluttered in any way.**

**WORK WITH COLOR**

In spaces visible from the entry, use contrasting colors that pull buyers in. If the distant walls are painted in cool colors—blues, greens, and grays—paint your front hall in a warm, complementary tone (see also Chapter Six). If the balance of your home has a mainly warm palette, paint your entry a moss green, pale gray, or blue. Use neutrals in varying tones to create a sense of warmth and cohesion and to capture the light in a dark space.

### Fifteen Entry Colors for Different Palettes

*Here are my favorite entry colors in the warm palette:*

❖ *Vivid Beauty (138)—orange tones*

❖ *Golden light (143)—yellow*

❖ *Florida Orange (153)*

❖ *Weston Flax (HC–5)*

❖ *Suntan Yellow (2155–50)*

*Here are my favorite entry colors in the cool palette:*

❖ *Yarmouth Blue (HC–150)*

❖ *Sherwood Green (HC–118)*

❖ *Rhine River (689)*

❖ *Catalina Blue (703)*

❖ *Baffin Island (243)*

*Finally, here are some good-choice neutral colors:*

❖ *Montgomery White (HC–33)*

❖ *Cottontail (2155–70)*

❖ *Sugar Cookie (2160–70)*

❖ *Abingdon Putty (HC–99)*

❖ *Acadia White (AC–41)*

## IMPRESSING YOUR TARGET BUYER

As you learned in Chapter One, not all buyers are created equal. This chapter cut across demographics to show you how to make a great first impression on *all* buyers, regardless of which generation they come from. However, you can and should also tailor your staging to the group of prospective buyers most likely to want your home. Here are some suggestions for staging your outside and indoor entry areas to specific target markets:

### If You're Targeting Baby Boomers

❖ Replace the plastic mailbox with a metal one.

❖ Tame any unruly garden beds.

❖ Have your bushes pruned by a professional.

❖ Replace cheap garage doors with fancy ones.

❖ Lay down an Oriental rug in the entryway.

❖ Hang a large gilt mirror in the hall.

### If You're Targeting Generation Jones

❖ Hang an American flag.

❖ Keep the wooden swing set.

❖ Repair and whitewash the fence.

❖ Resurface an asphalt walkway or driveway.

❖ Place a cedar bench in the yard or on the front porch.

❖ Seal coat the driveway.

### If You're Targeting Gen Xers

❖ Hang a framed concert poster or contemporary mirror in your front hall.

❖ Purchase colorful outdoor furniture.

❖ Plant a sustainable garden.

❖ Remove cute seasonal wreaths and other holiday decorations.

❖ Hide the outdoor hoses.

### If You're Targeting Gen Yers

❖ Minimize your existing garden.

❖ Paint your front door a bright color.

❖ Lay down an earth-friendly doormat.

❖ Organize your front hall closets.

❖ Strip all entryway wallpaper and repaint.

❖ Deformalize the entry.

## IF TIME AND MONEY ARE SHORT

Even if you need to spruce up your curb appeal in a hurry or if money is really tight right now, you can still improve prospective buyers' first impressions of your property by following these must-do steps.

> **Must-Do List for First Impressions**
>
> ❖ Be involved in the photo-taking process (see also Chapter Six).
>
> ❖ Make sure your realtor's sign is clean and straight.
>
> ❖ Wash your windows, inside and out.
>
> ❖ Prune your shrubbery so that it no longer blocks any windows or paths.
>
> ❖ If you have a yard or garden: weed, mulch, edge, and mow.
>
> ❖ Repaint your front door if possible; if not, clean it thoroughly.
>
> ❖ Remove anything cute, personal, political, or religious.
>
> ❖ Change your house or apartment numbers if they're old or out of style.

## THE NEXT STEP: CREATING SPACE

Now that you've spruced up the approach to your home and your inside entryway to appeal to your prospective buyers the minute they lay eyes on your property, you're ready to move farther inside. Before you can get to the artistic aspect of staging—in fact, before you can even clean your home for staging—you need to do an extremely thorough uncluttering. Chapter Three walks you through this crucial process step by step.

# Creating Space

*Simplicity is the ultimate sophistication.* —*Leonardo da Vinci*

**STRIPPED DOWN**, real estate is space: a little corner of the earth that you can call your own. Think of your property as a frame into which you put the artwork that is your life: your family, possessions, habits, and style. As long as you are living in the space defined by that frame, your life's artwork belongs there. But when you're enticing prospective buyers to fall in love with your property, you need to offer them enough space that they can easily imagine the artwork of their own lives fitting comfortably into that frame.

Buyers will focus on whatever you choose to leave inside the frame when you're showing your home. They will notice whether the space inside the frame feels generous or cramped, available or already occupied, friendly or alien. Give buyers enough space for their needs and dreams, furnish that space to reflect how they want their lives to be, and you will sell your home.

## TAKING THE "YOU" OUT OF YOUR HOME

All homes are defined by the owner's taste, and right now your home is filled with yours. Staging is the fine art of infusing your space with your most likely buyer's taste. To do this, as you learned in Chapter One, you must first take the "you" out of your property. Call it uncluttering, simplifying, weeding out—whatever you like—as long as you don't skip this crucial step. If you've been following the steps in the book so far, you've already found ways to say good-bye to your home, you've identified the generation(s) of buyers you're pursuing, and you've simplified and uncluttered the places that

*Figure 3–1. This previously unused space under a metal staircase now serves as a spatial vignette about aspiring to a lifestyle. The combination of a T'ang dynasty horse, contemporary art, and a small bar is likely to appeal most to Gen X buyers.*

prospective buyers will see as they approach and then enter your home, so that their first impressions will be good ones.

Uncluttering is even more important than identifying your target market, although the younger your prospective buyers, the less forgiving they will tend to be if you have not thoroughly removed the "you" from your home. This chapter walks you through the process of doing just that: creating space in the rest of your property.

## PREPACKING

With your past honored, your home's curb appeal boosted, and perhaps even some momentum built up in the packing department,

*Figure 3–2. Remove your own taste from the property by packing up your possessions. Give prospective buyers the space to visualize how they might like to live.*

you can move ahead with gusto. "Prepacking" is a gracious term for plain old uncluttering, and it is one of the most important steps in staging. You will need to prepack almost all your decorative arts. Your fabulous collections will distract buyers from your mission: making them fall in love with your property. Or if your buyers don't have your good taste, your things may just look like clutter. I know that is hard to believe, but it happens. You need to remove

*Figure 3–3.* **Before:** *"Clutter" seems like a coarse term for the decorative items in this pretty hallway, but their presence distracts the viewer from the hallway's architectural assets.*

all your collections and all your clutter because they both create the same thing in your home: an avoidable distraction. Pack them up and move them out. This is especially true when you're marketing your home to Gen Xers and Gen Yers, who cannot imagine ever accumulating that much stuff.

You cannot have a balanced room with clutter. You cannot have a welcoming, spacious, or visionary home with clutter.

For a more earthy perspective, imagine your child picking something up off the floor of your home. Maybe it's an old cracker, maybe it's a bit of clutter, but whatever it is, it's just family debris and you don't worry about it much. Now imagine your child or grandchild picking something up from the sidewalk. Ugh! What is that? Where has it been? Maybe it's safe to hold, but you snatch it away from your child just in case. Likewise, even prospective buyers who live in cluttered homes of their own will feel turned off by your clutter—simply because it's not theirs.

Finally, even though many of the world's most creative and successful people have done their best work in cluttered environments, the truth is that our society perceives people whose homes or work spaces are cluttered as somehow less successful, less able to manage their lives. Buyers, whether they are aware of it or not, prefer to buy a home from a successful person. So for the purposes of staging, you must unclutter.

Rent a storage space or borrow a friend's garage to store your items off

*Figure 3–4.* **After: Now that most the collections and artwork have been pre-packed, buyers can easily focus on the stairs and the beauty of the space.**

the premises. Don't be cheap and stack your boxes in the basement, garage, or attic. These are all parts of your property and need to be staged as well. If you stack your boxes in these places, you're not creating space in your home; you're just filling up different parts of it.

You need to minimize aggressively. One of my Transitional Tailors likes to equate living in

*Figure 3–5.* **Before: This empty hallway looks institutional. Buyers would have a hard time envisioning how to furnish this space to create an appealing feeling of home.**

### A Note About Storage Units

*Clients have carefully packed their family treasures and memorabilia and put it all into storage. When they pull it out six months later, they find it completely mildewed. If you rent a storage unit, make sure it's climate controlled! This goes for basement and attic space you might be renting or borrowing as well.*

a staged home to living in a hotel. Only keep with you what you need for the next month, and prepack or hide away all of your personal effects. In a city apartment, prepack 60 percent of your personal items. You can get away with about 50 percent in a large, suburban home. Yes, really: Prepack over half your items.

## WHY NOT SHOW YOUR HOME EMPTY?

Sellers often ask a very good question: "If space is what we're selling, why not show my property empty?" I offer two reasons for staging rather than merely emptying your home. First, empty homes seem smaller than staged

*Figure 3–6.* After: *Not only does this hallway seem larger when staged, but the institutional feeling is completely gone. Now buyers can imagine furnishing the hallway as part of their home.*

homes. (Oddly, so do homes whose rooms are crowded with furniture and small possessions.) Staged homes are designed to accentuate the space and to show prospective buyers how they might live in the home. This brings me to my second reason: Most people can't easily imagine what is not right in front of them. Unless your prospective buyers are designers, architects, or otherwise skilled in three-dimensional envisioning, the chances are that they'll have trouble visualizing what an empty room might look like furnished, what furniture might fit, and what might not.

Empty rooms and floor plans can fool buyers into creating unrealistic ideas for the space. I help many people downsize into continuing care or retirement facilities. Often, these facilities give their clients a floor plan of

*Figure 3–7.* **Before:** *Faced with this empty living room in a tony Philadelphia loft building, buyers would probably focus on the mechanics of the room, especially the exposed outlet.*

the client's new townhouse, apartment, or condominium. By the time I make my initial visit to clients, they have usually scribbled all kinds of wonderful ideas onto the floor plan. Their layouts are great, I explain, except that most of their friends have knees, which require more space between the coffee table and the sofa. Often my clients have placed the dining chairs smack up against a wall on the layout in an effort to squeeze their large dining room set into a smaller space. I applaud their efforts but point out that most of

*Figure 3–8.* After: *Staging the room gives it the feel of a successful, intelligent person's home. Buyers are enticed into imagining how they might arrange their own furniture in the same space.*

their friends are not flat and flexible like Gumby—the only type of dinner guest they could seat using their plan.

Open floor plans are the hardest to visualize. Walking into a large empty space, very few people can imagine how their furniture might look, much less fit. Staging gives the buyer a visual clue about how they might live in the space.

## If Uncluttering Seems Utterly Overwhelming

For many of us, keeping our possessions organized and letting go of things that have outlived their usefulness is a lifelong challenge. Piles of paper build up so quickly that we essentially give up on controlling them; we keep broken things around because we plan to fix them—but never find time; we loyally hang on to all the china handed down from our grandparents and the gifts from friends, even when they're clogging our sideboards and surfaces. Faced with uncluttering our entire home in a relatively short time, we feel anxious at best and completely paralyzed at worst.

This book is not intended to help clutter-challenged people figure out why they've always had trouble uncluttering, but if you are one of those people or you live with one, know that you are definitely not alone. Many sellers find that their enthusiasm for having their home staged for sale gives way to a feeling of increasing anxiety when they realize that they must deal comprehensively with their accumulated possessions and keep the home looking good for the buyers coming through. On the other hand, I often hear from clients that after our initial meeting they slept well for the first time in weeks. Why? Because they realized that my strategies for packing and organizing in bite-size portions would allow them to get their home ready on time for a strong sale.

### WHEN COUPLES DIFFER IN UNCLUTTERING ABILITY

In many couples trying to sell a home, there is one Decisive Prioritizer and one Unclutter Dreader. I grew up, as many of us did, as a child of one of these mixed marriages. My parents subscribed to about forty magazines and newspapers. My mother—the Decisive Prioritizer—would whip through her latest *New Yorker, Time, Antiques,* or *Newsweek,* and toss it. No back issue of any periodical of hers, whether daily, weekly, or monthly, ever cluttered her world. My father, on the other hand, was an Adult Unclutter Dreader. He had a home office whose pathways we navigated between waist-high piles of newspapers, magazines, and books—his personal open stack library. He would not allow a newspaper to go out the door unless he'd looked at the whole thing. Considering that we got *The New York Times, Hartford Courant,* and *The Wall Street Journal* daily, the waist-high piles in his library were no surprise.

Since not all of us are Decisive Prioritizers, here are some tips for helping the Adult Unclutter Dreader in your life, whether that person is your partner or you:

- ❖ Have all your packing supplies ready, including marker pens so that boxes can be clearly labeled before their contents are forgotten.

- ❖ Remind yourself or your partner that you are being asked only to prepack things, not to throw anything away.

- ❖ Keep a large trash bag close at hand during prepacking, just in case you or your partner does find something to throw out.

- ❖ Assign a plastic file box for storing anything that must be attended to immediately.

- ❖ Break down the task of prepacking into manageable chunks of space or time. Ask yourself or your partner to tackle a finite task: Unclutter the top of just one bureau, or prepack as much as possible in five minutes, in fifteen minutes, in one hour. Clear limits and a sense of control over a small project can help calm and motivate a Unclutter Dreader.

*Figure 3–9.* **Before:** *If you are wondering whether you need to unclutter, take a look at this living room. Everyone needs to unclutter to get their home to the staging level.*

❖ Keep reminding yourself or your partner that you are packing, not sorting. Inevitably some sorting will take place, but don't let an Adult Unclutter Dreader get mired in rereading old love letters or sifting through college photos. The goal is not to sort, but to sell your home.

*Figure 3–10.* **After:** *Now you can see the windows, a major feature of the room.*

❖ If your partner is the Adult Unclutter Dreader, no matter how much this aspect of his or her character has exasperated you in the past, tell yourself firmly to be kind and supportive. Remind yourself that your partner is already off balance from the specter of the move and is now being asked to eliminate comfortable old piles and pack away dusty treasures that were perfectly fine where they were (in your partner's opinion). Don't distress your partner further. Make things easy by offering to prepare five boxes for packing, for example. Empower your partner by asking him or her to set time limits. You can even ask if you can prepack your partner's things—not throw out, but prepack them. Emphasize that you will not throw away any of your partner's possessions unless you receive permission.

❖ Remove boxes from the premises as soon as they are packed, so that no Adult Unclutter Dreader will be tempted to reopen them.

### HELP CHILDREN UNCLUTTER

All children are hoarders, especially when they are stressed. Explain that you are prepacking their things to keep them safe. With three Unclutter Dreaders under age twelve in my own family, I can attest to the need to reassure children that *nothing* will be thrown out without their say-so. You will have to work alongside them. Help them sort through their toys and memorabilia, and don't expect them to be willing to let go of much of anything.

Explain to teens that their collages and posters on the walls are costing the family money and must be prepacked for now. I am not above bribery: If your teens can remove their personal shrines to those awkward years and keep their rooms tidy for showings, offer to buy them something that they want for their new room. A gift may be quite appropriate, in any case. Children feel powerless when their parents decide to sell their home, and their efforts to help with the move (even if halfhearted or resentful) should be recognized.

Small children are equally distressed and usually more scared. Often the only bedroom they know is the one they're being asked to give up. Help them to prepack their toys in readiness for their new rooms. Give them numbers to work with: How about if you keep out five favorite animals, six puzzles, and four games? Deviate from these arbitrary guidelines, and your children will feel that they have won something over on you; this is fine because they need to feel some sense of power in this situation. Prepacking with children always involves compromise. Keep reminding yourself, and them, what uncluttering strides you are making.

### A SILVER LINING TO THE STAGING PROCESS

For those of you who live with someone whose clutter tolerance is high and motivation to unclutter is low, the challenging work of uncluttering and staging may bring about an unexpected benefit. Often when the Adult Unclutter Dreader lives in a clutter-free space for a while, he or she begins to like it. Many of my clients find that they don't miss their clutter and collections, and when they finally get around to opening the boxes, they throw almost all of the contents away. This is what I call the aging clutter trick: Once the clutter is older, it becomes less important.

When we moved to Philadelphia, my husband packed all of his important ephemera—high school football plays, Japanese train passes, on and on—which had been housed in a whole corner of our basement. These twenty boxes went straight into our new basement. Several years later, when we moved again, he sorted through them. In two days, he was able to say good-bye to almost everything in those boxes. (Of course, this poor Adult Unclutter Dreader was living 24/7 with me, and I suspect that by the time he threw out his memorabilia, he was experiencing the clutter equivalent of Stockholm syndrome.)

### KEEP YOUR EYES ON THE PRIZE

Clutter costs money. This is not a book that teaches you how to organize your life, and I am not going to preach the emotional benefits of uncluttering. What I can tell you is this: Uncluttering will help you sell your home for the most money possible. Ask your realtor what a typical price reduction is for a property at your asking price if your home languishes on the market too long. It's probably anywhere from $5,000 to $50,000. Look around you. Is the luxury of having your clutter within reach worth this amount of money to you? Probably not. Remember, I'm not asking you to throw out your clutter. I am asking only that you prepack it. If you find that you can get rid of some things in the process, terrific. But packing your clutter and dealing with it later is a whole lot cheaper than allowing it to impede the sale of your property and your ability to move into the future.

Now let's get back to the nuts and bolts of prepacking.

> ### *Put a Price on Your Piles*
> *Try this trick to keep your eyes on the prize: On colorful sticky notes, in bold marker, write the price reduction amount your realtor is predicting if your home doesn't sell quickly enough. Place a note on each pile of clutter that you're having trouble packing up. (Do this before you put your home on the market, of course!) My clients find that doing this makes packing up that clutter a lot more appealing, and you may too.*

## EVERYTHING YOU NEED TO KNOW ABOUT BOXES

Buy professional moving boxes. They come in standard sizes that will be more efficient for you or the movers to use when the time comes. Fewer things inside them will be broken, and they will stack more easily. Some moving companies will refuse to move your possessions unless they're in professional moving boxes. Do not collect old boxes from the grocery or liquor store. These are not designed to move your belongings, and your things will inevitably break.

### WHAT BOXES TO USE

You'll need a variety of box sizes. Here are the ones that we use:

❖ *Book Boxes.* These small cartons (1.5 cubic feet, or 17 × 12⅜ × 12⅜ inches) are designed for heavy items, such as books, records, CDs, and canned goods. Don't pack books in anything bigger than these.

❖ *Legal Totes.* These boxes (2.3 cubic feet, or 24 × 16 × 13 inches) are specially designed for your files and folders.

❖ *Medium Boxes.* These boxes (3 cubic feet, or size 101/8 × 18 × 16 inches) are designed for nonfragile and moderately heavy items, such as pots, pans, linen, folded clothes, toys, and games.

❖ *Large Boxes.* These boxes (4.5 cubic feet, or 18 × 18 × 24 inches; and 6 cubic feet, or 23 × 23 × 20 inches) should be used for light, large, bulky items, such as pillows, comforters, and lamp shades.

❖ *Dish Packs.* These boxes (5.2 cubic feet, or 18 × 18 × 28 inches) have double, extra thick walls specifically designed for dishes, vases, glasses, and other fragile items. You can also use cell pack separators for china or glassware, with individual compartments for the items being packed.

**Figure 3–11. Packing your items properly in appropriate, professional moving boxes will save you breakage and heartache later.**

❖ *Mirror Boxes or Picture Boxes.* These narrow boxes accommodate different-size mirrors, paintings, and other fragile or flat items.

❖ *Wardrobe Boxes.* These boxes come equipped with a metal bar so that clothes can hang inside.

Contrary to common thinking, always fold your boxes without interlocking the four flaps on each side. Simply fold the two short opposite sides in and then the longer two opposite sides. Place tape across and on both sides on the outside. Tape the inside seam of the two flaps for added strength.

### SUPPLIES FOR PACKING

Buy packing supplies in bulk; you'll save time and money. You can even buy them online and have them delivered to your home. That's one less errand to run! Here's what you'll need:

❖ *Tape.* The most common tape used for carton sealing is a plastic tape called PVC. Buy at least twelve rolls to start.

❖ *Newsprint.* This is newsprint, not newspaper. Never use newspapers as wrapping material. Newspaper ink has a tendency to rub off on the items it touches and is very difficult to remove from fine china. Instead, use newsprint paper—the inexpensive, off-white paper that newspapers are printed on (you can find it at any art store)—as cushioning material.

❖ *Tissue Paper.* Use this to pack up delicate items by layering tissue over and over.

❖ *Bubble Wrap or Packing Peanuts.* We prefer bubble wrap; it's easier to control. Besides, your children will love squishing or stomping on the bubbles so that you can pack to a fusillade of bubble wrap artillery noises. (Think of the alternative: your children and billions of packing peanuts. Don't go there.)

❖ *Ziploc® Bags.* These can be used for packing small assortments of items like medicines or miscellaneous contents of containers and drawers.

❖ *Magic or Permanent Markers.* Use these for labeling boxes.

❖ *Scissors or Utility Blades.*

> ### *How to Label Boxes*
> *Here's the information each box should have on it, to save you time and*
> *trouble later:*
>
> ❖ *Which room it came from*
>
> ❖ *Which room it should go in*
>
> ❖ *Whether it is fragile*
>
> ❖ *Whether it should be loaded last so that it will be unloaded first*
>
> ❖ *What's inside it (a packing summary)*

Think of prepacking as getting a jump on the moving process. In addition to removing distracting items from the property, prepacking helps to reduce clutter, to create an environment that is easier to clean and keep clean, and to lessen your packing burden. You cannot successfully analyze the space in a room or home until you can see it. Here's how to tackle this Herculean task.

## OUT WITH THE PERSONAL AND POSSIBLY CONTENTIOUS

The intimate flavor of your home—where the "you" is most evident—is revealed most strongly in your personal and partisan possessions. Accordingly, removing these items is crucial to the staging process because, if you leave them in sight, you risk distracting or even offending your prospective buyers.

### REMOVING OBJECTS WITH POSSIBLY CONTENTIOUS AFFILIATIONS

Remove anything that signifies a political, religious, sports, or school association. (This includes your wall of fame—that is, your diplomas, awards, bowling trophies, and so on—if you have one.) Even if you suspect a prospective buyer will share your politics or your religion, any expression of allegiance to a group that doesn't include all prospective buyers will narrow your market. To put it simply, anything that speaks specifically to one group of people—whether it's a Mets cap on a coat hook, a statue of the Madonna in the garden, or a mezuzah at the door— will exclude any buyer who does not feel a part of that group. Your goal, when staging, is to have potential buyers walk through your home imagining your property as theirs.

### REMOVING ALL PHOTOGRAPHS AND PORTRAITS

Prepack all your personal pictures. Pictures only remind people that this is your home, not theirs. When we're working on a property, we often go through the whole home, pull all the family photos, and pack them in the same box. When clients are unpacking, they can then see the pictures anew as they arrange them in their new home.

Even if prospective buyers find your personal pictures as appealing as you do (which is not at all a sure thing), your pictures will distract them from the features of your property. You don't want buyers to get waylaid looking at your photos instead of your wainscoting. Don't complicate buyers' lives by triggering the memory that they coached your child in Little League or that they know your mother from synagogue.

> ### Items with Written Sayings Are Taboo
> Remove anything with a written saying on it. Deep-six the needlepoint pillow that says "Mirror, Mirror, on the wall, I am my mother after all"; the little wooden sign in the garden that says "Cat lover lives here"; the sign in the kitchen that says "More loving, less cooking." You would remove bumper stickers before trying to sell your car, wouldn't you? Do the same thing for your property. Nothing will remind a buyer more that the property is yours, not theirs, than these little witticisms.

## DECIDING WHAT FURNITURE AND RUGS TO REMOVE

Count the pieces of furniture in each room and plan to reduce that number by one-third. Your rooms will feel empty to you, but your buyers will think that they look open and airy. Remove all but four chairs from the kitchen table. In the dining room, remove leaves from the table (if any) until only six chairs fit comfortably around it. You may leave two chairs against the walls in the dining room if you have the space. Plan to remove any furniture that blocks a window in any way or that sits within three feet of a door.

If you can, take away the extra desk space that you've added to your desk area. In the best-case scenario, this means the desk return that was designed for your desk; in the worst case scenario, this means the printer table you found on the street, the extra tables you have laid out around your desk, and so on. I find that home offices often have a virtual maze of additional desk space made up of desk returns, card tables, and any other horizontal surface the Adult Unclutter Dreader has been able to annex from the mainstream life of the home.

In children's rooms, remove the nursing rocker and its footstool. They are ugly and almost always too big for the room.

Often I walk into a home and find furniture lining the walls of a room like wallflowers at a dance. Slate these sideliners for removal. You are selling the walls, not the chairs, but you can't sell the walls if your prospective buyers can't see them. Plan to remove all tables that do not directly service a chair. With few exceptions, hallways should be clear of furniture.

### REMOVING FREESTANDING BOOKCASES AND ENTERTAINMENT CENTERS

Freestanding bookcases and entertainment centers almost always overpower a room. Not only do they ruin the proportions of the room, they're also usually out of plumb with the wall they stand against. The advent of the flat-screen TV has made entertainment centers outdated. Your used bookshelves and entertainment center—even your Chippendale-style TV cabinet—will have little resale value, and you're probably better off just taking them to the curb.

### REMOVING RUGS THAT ARE TOO STAINED OR TOO SMALL FOR THE SPACE

Don't leave any stained rugs in your home while your property is on the market. Area rugs often skew the balance in a home. They make a space look cluttered and smaller and are often a tripping hazard. Empty floors look better than a scattering of small rugs that obviously do not fit the

*Figure 3–12.* **Before: This front hall area is so cluttered that the viewer doesn't know where to look. Note the random furniture items that need to be removed (see "Furniture and Rugs to Remove").**

room. If you can afford it, buy a rug that fits the room. Find a carpet rem-
nants store, and have a neutral tan, wool, or sisal rug cut and finished that
will lie about 6 inches from the wall all the way around the room. For
instance, for a 12 × 15 foot room, have an 11 × 14 foot rug cut. Steer
away from patterns. Don't make a statement with your rug; you want the

*Figure 3–13.* **After: Uncluttered, the front hall
area is far more restful
visually, and the archi-
tecture stands out.**

rug to blend into the room. Ask the store to bind or serge the edge in the same color as the rug because a contrasting perimeter breaks up the room visually.

> ### Furniture and Rugs to Remove
> 
> *These types of furnishings tend to crowd your rooms and should be removed:*
> 
> ❖ *Armoires*
> 
> ❖ *Baskets*
> 
> ❖ *Clothes racks*
> 
> ❖ *Filing cabinets*
> 
> ❖ *Folding screens*
> 
> ❖ *Freestanding bookcases*
> 
> ❖ *Magazine stands*
> 
> ❖ *Nursing rockers and footstools*
> 
> ❖ *Ottomans*
> 
> ❖ *Desk returns*
> 
> ❖ *Printer tables and the like*
> 
> ❖ *Side chairs without a desk or table*
> 
> ❖ *Small area rugs that don't add to their space*
> 
> ❖ *Trunks*
> 
> ❖ *TV cabinets and entertainment centers*

### REMOVING SELECTED FURNITURE AND RUGS

For staging purposes, the furniture that you've selected for removal is clutter. Clutter costs, so these items need to be moved off the premises. First, of course, you must prepack everything that is in or on those furnishings. Put on some great music, ask a friend to help you, make some strong coffee—do whatever it takes to get through the work of prepacking. When you think you can't prepack one more box, review the advice under "If Uncluttering Seems Utterly Overwhelming."

For the furnishings, rent a storage unit if you have to (remember what I said about climate control), or have your movers do a preliminary pickup and store the extra furnishings until you move. Do not store them in the basement or garage. Stacking furniture there not only indicates to the buyer that your property is too small, but also ruins the effect of such areas, which are often strong selling points for a home.

> ### *Cleaning and Moving Rugs and Draperies*
> *Have any rugs and draperies you're not using for staging cleaned before moving. If a rug is still stained after cleaning it, don't use it for staging. Often, cleaners will pick up at the old address and deliver to your new address, either gratis or for a nominal fee. You can have rugs delivered a day before the main move, so the rugs are laid and ready to go.*

## CLEARING THE DECKS AND THE DEPTHS: ADVANCED UNCLUTTERING

Now that you've gotten things off the walls and have thinned out your furnishings, it's time to attend to the rest of the small stuff that's peppering the surfaces in your home and clogging your drawers and closets. In this section, you'll find specific advice for uncluttering each part of your property.

### UNCLUTTERING ALL LATERAL SURFACES

Never forget: You are not selling your things; you are selling space. Your things will distract prospective buyers from seeing the space. Remove all items from the mantelpieces and window sills. Remove all that you can from the kitchen counters (no small feat). Remove decorative collections, statues, and doilies. Prepack all your mementos from trips: the puppets, masks, dancing figurines, Dutch clogs, and so on. All house plants should leave the premises during staging. They take up crucial lateral space and usually don't add to the ambience of the home. Occasionally we make an exception for a very healthy floor plant that is at least three feet high and in a ceramic pot or for an orchid to liven up a stagnant space. (For advice on staging with flowers, see Chapter Six.) You've already removed all your family photos, right? Pack everything up, label the boxes, and get them off your property.

### TACKLING CLOSETS AND DRAWERS

I recently staged a home for a lovely, sophisticated woman who was panicked that people would be looking through the drawers of her breakfront china cabinet. She actually thought that buyers could look through all her drawers. Buyers have every right to open any drawers or closets that are *physically attached* to your home: built-in cabinets and closets, built-in kitchen and bathroom drawers. They *do not* have the right to open (much less look through) any drawers of your freestanding furniture or into your freestanding armoires (but those should be gone anyway). As the cleaning lady listening to our conversation said to my client: "They start looking through your bureau, I'm calling the cops." Stuff your dresser or china cabinet drawers as full as you want. Just realize that you're going to have to pack it all later.

In this section, I'm talking about the closets and drawers that are fair game for prospective buyers to open as they evaluate how much closet space the home has, how easily the kitchen drawers slide, and so on. In these cases, you must clean out at least 50 percent of what's in every closet and drawer.

I find that many of my clients get so revved up about uncluttering that they start tackling the drawers in their freestanding furniture as well. This is great, but only if you've already packed away all your visible clutter and after you have sorted and cleaned all built-in drawers and cabinets. Tackle uncluttering your built-in drawers first.

Prepack all your off-season clothes. Leave your closets half full. The coat closet is one of the most important places to clear. Coat closets are invariably too small. They're also usually in the front hall, and buyers will see them while still forming their initial reaction to your home. Review Chapter Two to make sure you've done all you can to create a fabulous first impression for prospective buyers.

Empty your kitchen drawers and cabinets as best you can. Get rid of anything that you don't want to pay to move. Empty your cabinets of all but the absolutely necessary food, pots and pans, utensils, and china. Remember that old canned goods, extra Tupperware, paper bags, and the like all cost money to move. Are they worth it?

### CLEARING HALLWAYS

First, because *buyers' first impressions are so important*, remember what we said in Chapter Two about the entry to your home, and do not skimp on your efforts to make their first impressions positive ones.

If the front hallway can accommodate a small table for keys and mail as well as a chair or bench and still provide 36 inches of passing room, these are welcome additions. If you do not have at least 36 inches in which to maneuver, remove the furniture. All other hallways need to be clear and light and clean. Remove the small tables, the chairs that serve no purpose, and the desk that never gets used.

### UNCLUTTERING MUDROOMS AND VESTIBULES

These spaces are like hall closets on steroids. If yours is in the front entrance to your home, you've dealt with it already in Chapter One. But if your back door leads into a mudroom, for example, be sure to unclutter that room with a vengeance. Just retain the bare minimum your family needs in the way of outerwear, footwear, backpacks, and sports equipment during the selling process. Remember, you want your buyers to decide that your home has *plenty* of storage space.

### UNCLUTTERING THE KITCHEN

Kitchens are often the psychic heart of a property, unless the home is a tiny apartment with an even tinier kitchen. But even tiny kitchens are where the

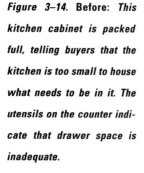

*Figure 3–14.* **Before:** *This kitchen cabinet is packed full, telling buyers that the kitchen is too small to house what needs to be in it. The utensils on the counter indicate that drawer space is inadequate.*

owners get sustenance, and larger kitchens are where buyers want to imagine entertaining and enriching their families and friends. The kitchen table is where most of the memorable family conversations happen. Because of all the time we spend in our kitchens, they tend to be hot spots for clutter. Calendars, lists, soccer schedules, magnets with the vet's phone number, watercoolers, and throw rugs clutter these rooms, which are already smaller

*Figure 3–15.* After: *These cabinets now are a successful, organized part of a large, country kitchen. The items on top of the cabinets and fridge are gone; the cabinet interior is uncluttered with no objects stacked on top of each other; the fridge magnets are gone; and the counter has been attractively staged.*

than their actual dimensions because of all the built-in cabinetry. Kitchens always look crowded.

Clear out as much as possible in the kitchen. Take the magnets and dry cleaning receipts off the fridge, untape the notes from the walls, prepack the cookbooks on the window sill, remove or store the remarkable cold cereal selection that graces the top of your fridge. Sort through the cabinets, and empty out all the canned goods and dried foods that have been there for more than a year. They'll cost more money to move than what they cost originally, and you'll probably never eat them if you haven't already. If they're still within their sell-by date, give them to a soup kitchen. Clear out at least 50 percent of the contents of any open or glass-fronted cabinets.

Sort through your pots and pans and get rid of any that are burnt, scratched, duplicated, or otherwise not worth moving. Prepack as much as you can: Leave only the dishes that you need for the next few months. Pack up the punch bowl and the lobster pot. Your goal is to make your kitchen seem spacious, not crowded. You can use some of this newfound cabinet and drawer space to store the items that currently clutter the counter. Remove or store all the small appliances that you can: portable microwaves, toasters, electric can opener. They all eat up counter space. Leave only what you need for daily use. You will be amazed at how appealing your counters look when you're done.

### UNCLUTTERING BATHROOMS

Bathrooms need to be pristine. Besides being prime clutter territory, they are a hot spot for too much information. Sort through your medicine cabinet. Throw out any medications, cleansers, and makeup whose time is past. Unless you bought towels in the last year, throw out your old towels and buy new white ones. Because potential buyers will be looking in all your bathroom cabinets, store your makeup, prescription medications, and anything else you don't want strangers to see in travel kits below the counter for privacy.

Leave as little on countertops as possible, and nothing decorative. Take everything off the back of the toilet, the top of the medicine cabinet, and the window sills, and recycle that big pile of magazines. Now that you've freed up some space in the medicine cabinet, you might put a few of your daily cleansing and shaving items inside it. But remember: Buyers want to imagine themselves in your home. Their desire to use their imagination will come to a hard stop in the bathroom if they see your Lactaid and Nair. Don't spoil their dreams! Pack up your personal items.

### UNCLUTTERING YOUR HOME OFFICE

A home office is rarely uncluttered. Clear off the desktop. Your buyer wants to imagine working at this desk, not slowly sifting through reams of paper and bills to pay. Pack your snow globe collection, your old desk identifier from two jobs ago, your Big Apple Conference paperweight, everything that you possibly can. Some of my clients have so many office supplies that their workspace looks like a Staples satellite. Prepack it all, except for what you will need in the next three months. You will survive. If you run out of sticky notes, you can buy another pack.

You already know that filing cabinets, freestanding bookshelves, desk returns, and printer tables should be removed if possible. Add the plastic floor mat for the desk chair to that list. Your wall of fame should be prepacked as well. Keep one file drawer or plastic file box of active files that you cannot do without for the next three months.

### UNCLUTTERING THE DINING ROOM AND LIVING ROOM

Pack all your tasteful collectibles, crystal, silver, wedding gifts, and the like. Clear your mantelpiece and window sills and remove any sheer blinds, unless you are looking at an awful view or right into a neighboring apartment. Prepack at least 50 percent of the visible contents of glass-fronted cabinets.

### UNCLUTTERING BOOKCASES

Unclutter any remaining bookshelves. For staging purposes, only about 60 percent—less than two-thirds—of a bookcase should contain books. If your bookshelves are full, count your books. Once again, take out your calculator. To achieve the 60 percent goal, multiply the number of books by 0.6. This is the number of books that you may keep in the bookcase. For example, if you have 350 books in a bookcase, you must prepack or get rid of 140 of them. This is easier than you think if you follow the next pieces of advice.

First, remove all paperbacks and pack up any that you want to take with you. Pack or recycle all encyclopedias, textbooks, political books, religious books, war books, sex books (you'd be surprised—or maybe not—how many sex books some homeowners have buried in the recesses of their bookshelves), and exercise books. As you're debating which books to keep and which to get rid of, please remember that they are heavy and cost a lot to move. Any books that you're not going to read again should be culled as well. Books can be donated to the local library or to a benefit book fair. Remove any books that extend beyond the shelf because they make the shelf look inadequate.

**Figure 3–16.** Before: *This bookcase is overcrowded and cluttered. Remove more than half of the books, all the photos, and leave only one type of decorative item.*

## UNCLUTTERING BEDROOMS

Remove as much as you can. Like bathrooms, bedrooms can reveal way too much about their owners. Your buyers don't even want to think about you in these rooms, any more than you want to go to a hotel room and wonder who slept there last.

Making up your beds with plain bedding and white sheets and pillow-cases, rather than patterned or colored bed linens, will make bedrooms seem larger and is a good way to take the "you" out of this intimate space.

Clear your surfaces. Put away the jewelry boxes, the candy dishes, the ear-ring tree, the family pho-tos, the clocks, the change bowl, and so on.

Put the exercise bike in storage rather than in its place of honor in the bedroom corner. By age thirty—the average age of a first-time home buyer, remember—one hopes to

*Figure 3–17.* **After: Look at the difference. The shelves seem larger, the three pewter ornaments are easier on the eye, and the chair has been moved to open up the view to the fireplace.**

### Packing Books

*Pack books tightly on end in small boxes. If the books smell musty, sprinkle talcum powder between their pages and wrap each book individually in tissue paper before packing. Leave them stored this way for a couple of months to eliminate the smell.*

have graduated from staring at the pedal of an exercise bike while going to sleep. You want your bedroom to be simultaneously relaxing, neutral, and inviting.

### UNCLUTTERING GUEST ROOMS, SEWING ROOMS, AND MULTIPURPOSE ROOMS

Guest rooms almost always seem smaller than they are. They frequently become catch-all rooms for unfinished projects, sewing experiments, off-season clothing, and other items that tell prospective buyers that the home does not have enough space. Clean out the guest room closet and remove all those other projects.

### UNCLUTTERING THE LAUNDRY AREA

Oddly, this place in the home, where the clothes get cleaned, is often quite unpresentable. Dryer fluff accumulates in the corners; old half-full bottles of detergent and softener gather on shelves or dryer tops, creating soapy rings. Some of us have amassed several lint rollers from our dry cleaners as gifts; pack these away. For now, recycle or combine any extra bottles of detergent, if possible. Just keep the bare minimum of supplies that you need on hand. If nonlaundry-related items have somehow ended up piled on your dryer or clogging the shelves nearby, remove them.

### MANAGING PETS AND THEIR PARAPHERNALIA

Ideally, you want no evidence of pets in the home, especially in apartments and other close quarters. If you can, remove your pets from the home during the sale process. We recently staged a home for a family with three cats that used the attached garage as their litter box. Ridding the garage of the smell of cat urine required several thousands of dollars of remediation.

Pets are tricky elements in the equation of selling your home. Let's face it: As much as we love them, they tend to be dirty and smelly, and—like dreams—they're often not as interesting or endearing to others as they are to their owners. Especially in this age of aggravated allergies, the best pet when staging your home is no pet. If you must keep your pet in the home during the sales process, remove its food and water bowls during showings, and crate your pet or keep it safely penned outside if possible. Clean the litter box twice a day while your home is on the market, and change the litter completely twice a week. Wash the dog bed and brush your dogs outside daily to minimize hair and dander.

### UNCLUTTERING PORCHES AND PATIOS

Porches and patios should be swept clean (don't forget to sweep away cobwebs under a porch roof) and weeded, if necessary. Remove any furniture other than some charming outdoor furniture that matches and that doesn't overcrowd the space, if you have it. Take down hanging plants, wind chimes, and other ornaments. Pack away the children's toys that have ended up on your porches.

### UNCLUTTERING BASEMENTS, GARAGES, AND OUTBUILDINGS

Basements, garages, and outbuildings such as barns and workshops are luxuries. They're often the most overlooked parts of a property, yet they can be some of the most treasured places in a home. Historically considered the domain of the male, these are spaces where you can experiment, create, or play. They can be tremendous selling features, but they are catch-alls.

Except for a small washer/dryer area that my mother tried to maintain, my father held sway over our basement. Cheek by jowl down there were two extra fridges, an arts and crafts worktable for my sister and me, old marine patents of my grandfather's, my father's workbench, two dollhouses, an orchid room, a wine cellar, a jerry-rigged photo lab, four or five old sets of china, three train sets—and all that is just what comes to mind some thirty years later. Our basement was a luxury, a place for dreaming and creating, a jungle to explore as a child and as an adult. The space was amazing. Unfortunately, no one could see it because of all the clutter. As you decide what to dispose of, prepack, or leave for staging in your own basement, garage, or other outbuildings, think about creating that feeling of luxurious, extra, private space for your prospective buyers and their dreams.

Back to brass tacks. Many of the materials not allowed in a moving van are stored in the basement and garage. A partial list of these hazardous items follows (see "Things That Are Too Hazardous to Pack"), but check with your movers and then with your municipality to find out how to dispose of these items. My suggestion is to err on the side of caution and safely dispose of anything that might break, spill, or blow up the moving truck. I remember that when I moved in with my husband, I brought a white sofa, onto which was packed a box of my kitchen items. The red wine vinegar—total cost, perhaps $3—broke and leaked all over my white sofa. Life is full of these ironies. At least it wasn't a flammable liquid.

### Things That Are Too Hazardous to Pack

- Acid
- Ammonia
- Ammunition
- Batteries
- Car batteries
- Charcoal
- Chemistry sets
- Cleaning fluid
- Fertilizer
- Fireworks
- Gasoline
- Kerosene
- Lamp Oil
- Lighter fluid
- Liquid bleach
- Loaded weapons
- Matches
- Motor oil
- Nail polish and remover
- Paint thinner
- Paints
- Pesticides
- Poisons
- Pool chemicals
- Propane tanks
- Sterno aerosols
- Weed killer

REVISITING YOUR CLUTTER HOT SPOTS

Every home has spots that are the hardest to unclutter and maintain. The home office, the dining room table, and the kitchen counter are frequently culprits. Figure out where your worst clutter centers are and deal with them daily, especially every morning before you walk out the door. You know only too well how fast clutter builds up in these spots. Be vigilant in sorting every paper that comes into your home during the selling process. If you have a drawer below or near these clutter areas, try to empty it so that those fast-growing piles can at least be stored out of sight in an orderly fashion.

---

### *The Basket and How to Use It*

*I often suggest that my clients get a nice basket with a handle in which to place their clutter. Remember, you're looking for ways to function realistically while your property is on the market. You still need to be able to manage your needs. A clutter basket can be carried from the bedroom to the desk to the kitchen or anywhere you need to work with the items inside it. This is where you can put items to go to the car, mail to go out, bills to be paid, school permission slips, and so on. Check it every morning and evening when your home is on the market. If your clutter can be contained in one basket, you have conquered your clutter. Ideally, you can find room in an under-the-counter cabinet to hide your basket during showings.*

---

## DOUBLE-CHECKING YOUR UNCLUTTERING THROUGH A CAMERA LENS

Photographs—or even just looking through a camera lens—have the magical ability to reveal things that have become invisible to you because you're so used to them. Cameras tend to capture more than is visible to the naked eye. Photographs accentuate clutter, confusion, and any jarring items: a frayed electrical cord, a missing bathroom tile, a cluster of knickknacks on a shelf— all of the objects that become invisible to the naked eye are suddenly visible through the lens and in the resulting photograph. As you walk through your entire property, using your camera lens as a kind of magnifying glass, remove any smaller objects that jump to your attention and make note of where you need to clean and repair things, because that's what we going to tackle in the next chapter. If you take photographs during this walk-through, examine them as well to see what you might have missed.

## RECOGNIZING WHAT YOU HAVE ACCOMPLISHED

If you've been working along with my text, you have conquered the most emotionally intense part of the staging process: letting go. You have said your good-byes to your home, and you have prepacked and minimized like a pro. Was all that grueling prepacking worth it? Yes, it was. First of all, if you're serious about moving, you're going to have to pack your clutter at some point. It might as well be before you put your home on the market, so that you don't end up paying for your clutter in the form of a lower sales price.

Your home doesn't feel like it's yours anymore. That is a very good thing. We want it to feel that way. You are selling space, not your taste. Your property probably feels inadequately furnished. You probably don't like the way it looks now. That is also a good thing. Remember, you liked it back when it was your home, tailor-made for you. Now you're tailoring your property to fit the dreams of prospective buyers.

## IF TIME AND MONEY ARE SHORT

I recognize that you may not have the time or money to fully unclutter, much less stage your home. What follows is a must-do list that takes no money and not much time. You will be amazed at how much bigger your home will seem when you remove these items. Remember, I am not asking you to throw them out. Just move them out of your home so that you boost your chances for a strong sale.

Your belongings are clutter to prospective buyers. You want to help buyers envision living in your home. Clutter costs; uncluttering sells. Keep your eyes on the prize: avoiding that $5,000 to $50,000 price reduction. It is a lot of money to lose that you don't have to lose.

> ### *Must-Do List for Creating Space*
>
> ❖ *Clear horizontal surfaces of collections and papers.*
>
> ❖ *Clear all windows of furniture that block them, and clear items from the sills.*
>
> ❖ *Remove furniture in hallways.*
>
> ❖ *Remove sheer curtains (unless your view is an elevator shaft or a grave-yard—you get the picture).*
>
> ❖ *Remove all reference books and paperbacks.*
>
> ❖ *Remove all off-season clothing.*
>
> ❖ *Remove all personal photographs and items with political, religious, sports, or school affiliations.*
>
> ❖ *Remove all baskets, trunks, screens, magazine stands, ottomans, side chairs that do not have a desk or table, clothes racks, and small area rugs.*
>
> ❖ *If you can, remove all of the following: TV cabinets, any TVs that are not flat screen, freestanding bookcases, filing cabinets, printer tables, and desk returns.*

## The Next Step: Fixing and Cleaning

By simplifying and uncluttering your home to reveal its potential space, you are enabling buyers to fall in love with it. Your next step, taken in Chapter Four, is to cast a critical eye on all this newfound space, repair what needs repairing (on your own or with professional help), and clean your home as it has never been cleaned before.

# What to Fix and How to Clean

*Opportunity is missed by most people because it is dressed in overalls and looks like work.* —*Thomas Alva Edison*

**MAKING REPAIRS** and cleaning your home are crucial tasks that you must do no matter who your prospective buyers are. Functionality and cleanliness transcend generational taste barriers; not too many home buyers put busted window latches and black furry tile grout on their list of must-haves. We'll focus on generational preferences in the next two chapters, after you learn tips for making your home clean and whole in a way that it may have never been. You need to present your property to look as pristine as is humanly possible.

Now, you may be one of those people with a refrigerator magnet that says: "A clean house is the sign of a wasted life." If you are, you may be tempted to skip this chapter. Don't do it. You are needlessly minimizing the appeal of your property. Remember all the dust bunnies and nail holes in plaster walls that were revealed during the uncluttering process? (If you haven't uncluttered yet, make sure you're sitting down and review Chapter Three.) I can assure you that an extremely clean property is going to bring you more money than a dirty one or even a fairly clean one. And a well maintained home is going to bring you a lot more. You will be surprised how much more. In this chapter, we'll begin with repairs and move on to cleaning.

*Figure 4–1.* **Before:** *Cracks like this are common in wood or plaster, especially in older homes. Even though this crack is probably harmless, it should be repaired with spackle and a paint touch-up.*

## How Do You Know What to Fix?

Realtors have a saying: "Your buyer notices more in two minutes in your home than you've noticed in two years." This adage is alarming but true. Quite possibly, you haven't repaired some of what needs to be fixed because you haven't even noticed the problem. What you need are fresh eyes looking at your property.

## DO A WALK-THROUGH WITH AN OBSERVANT OUTSIDER

Once you've successfully said good-bye to your property (review Chapter One if you haven't done this), ask your realtor to do a critical walk-through with you. If you don't have a realtor, ask someone who will be straight with you in a constructive but not overly polite way. This should be someone obser- vant, preferably from the same generation as the buyers you hope to entice. Tell this person: "I've been reading *Home Staging That Works*, and I understand how much staging is going to affect my sales price. I want you to be brutally honest with me about what

*Figure 4–2.* After: *Now the door is whole again, so that it won't raise any nagging little worries for prospective buyers.*

I should change in my home to sell it fast and for the best price." Suggest that this person open and close doors, built-in cabinets and drawers, and windows. Have the observer turn on faucets, flush toilets, and do anything that potential buyers might do when touring your home. Then, during the actual walk-through, *you need to clam up*. Don't look hurt, no matter what feedback you get. Keep smiling and nodding encouragingly so that you get every last thought about how your home is not currently appealing to prospective buyers, and take good notes as you go around the house. No excuses and no "Yes, but . . ." should emanate from your lips. Remember, you asked for this feedback because it's going to help you sell your property.

You can even ask a friend or family member to take photos. This can provide a diplomatic way for people to alert you to things that have always bugged them about your home, without their having to come right out and say, "Gosh, that rug is filthy," or "Have you ever cleaned this bathtub?" or "Could you maybe fix this broken step *now?*" Rest assured, your prospective buyers will notice all the same things.

### GET A PREINSPECTION

Ask your realtor for the name of a highly reputable home inspector and hire the person to perform a preinspection. An average home inspection costs about $400 (prices vary depending on the part of the country and the size of the home), but if the inspector has a good reputation, the price is well worth paying. If you hire someone that no one's heard of, your preinspection might not be worth the paper it's written on. A preinspection is a message to prospective buyers that you are hiding nothing from them. In fact, you've brought in an inspector to assure them that nothing is amiss. A preinspection will help your property sell faster. You should include copies of this report with your marketing pieces for buyers to take home and peruse.

If your inspector flags a major issue, have the problem remedied and get a detailed receipt stating that the issue has been resolved. Don't scrimp and use Bud's Fly-by-Night Fixomatic for this. It pays to use the dominant vendor in the area. If you can't afford to have the problem fixed, get a written, detailed estimate from the best-known vendor and include this with the report. This will assure your buyer that the problem is solvable for a set cost. If your roof clearly needs repairs but you don't provide buyers with a professional estimate, they'll make an unprofessional, anxiety-based guesstimate mentally, usually for more than the repair would actually cost. Then they'll either walk away or deduct this guesstimate from their offering bid. Getting an estimate will save you from being gouged in negotiations. For example, I had clients who discovered via a preinspection that their home had no septic system or sewer line—a finding that was a bit disturbing in a close neighborhood in a watershed area. Something like this costs about $50,000 to remediate. The client couldn't afford to fix the problem, but they got a detailed estimate. Their realtor let prospective buyers know that they were offering a $50,000 credit based on that estimate.

If your home inspection reveals a major issue, ask your realtor to market the fact that you are offering to credit the buyer a certain amount of money toward the remediation. Again, this shows that you have nothing to hide; furthermore, it takes the negotiation over the issue off the table. This is not the moment to dig a trench to the sewer system or to climb up on the roof and do it yourself. Seeing a report that the roof needed fixing and then learning that the handy owner went up and replaced the shingles will strike fear into the heart of any buyer. If you're handy with tools, your home probably has many smaller repair issues that you can and should tackle. Focus on those! Leave the work detailed in the inspection report to the professionals.

> ### Repairs May Be Deductible
> *Often, you can take the cost of repairs toward the sale of a property as a tax deduction. Talk to a tax specialist about your particular situation to see if the expense is deductible.*

## WHY YOU CAN'T JUST IGNORE WHAT'S BROKEN

You've heard it before, and now you'll hear it from me: There is no such thing as deferred maintenance. You will pay for that broken fence post, ripped screen, or leaky faucet at closing, either explicitly in a line item that requires you to repair the issue or implicitly in a lower sales price. If you can fix these things yourself, you'll save yourself time and money. A property in poor condition scares away first-time buyers, because they've never had to handle or pay for repairs. Ironically, that same property scares away experienced homeowners as well, because they know how expensive and time-consuming repairs can be. So, if you can fix what needs fixing in your home before putting it on the market, do so. If you can't afford to fix something, at least disclose to your prospective buyers that the problem exists and give them a professional estimate on the repair cost, if possible.

## COMMONLY NEEDED REPAIRS

Not having seen your home, I'm going to run through a list of common problems; most of the properties we stage have these repair issues. Many of them don't come up in an inspection report and can be addressed by even the most wrench-averse seller. We'll begin by looking at typical exterior problems.

### YARDS AND GARDENS

If you haven't already followed the advice about yards and gardens in Chapter Two, review it now. In a nutshell, make sure your yard, shrubs, and garden are pruned, weeded, mulched, edged, and mowed. No plants or shrubs should block a window or encroach on a pathway. In dry areas, keep your plants well watered. You want your home to resemble an oasis.

### GUTTERS AND DOWNSPOUTS

Check your gutters and downspouts for leaks. Make sure that your gutter system channels rainwater well away from the house. You can generally fix these problems yourself with gutter patches and downspout extenders. If the ground where the gutter pours water is eroded, lay down some river rocks. They look better than a muddy mess and may help stop the erosion.

I was bringing tile samples to a client one rainy February day. As I stood on his front porch waiting for him to answer the door, I looked down. Two feet away was a downspout gushing water into a large puddle, which was in turn drenching the foundation. When my client opened the door, I mentioned that this waterfall could be causing real issues below ground. He said that he and his wife had had it looked at but didn't know what to do. I felt I might as well throw the tiles right into the puddle because that was the kind of money they were going to end up spending on remediation. And what an easy fix. But when it's not raining, you don't think about what your downspouts are doing. Trust me, people will be looking at your home in the rain. Tour the outside of your home the next time it rains, if possible. Take a good hard look in any case, and fix your downspouts now so that you don't have major foundation issues later.

### ROOFS

You are best off leaving roof repairs to the professionals. What you can do is to note anything you see that needs repair on the roof itself, as well as any areas where water seems to be coming into the home, any places where interior paint is peeling or forming bubbles, and any rooms (including the basement) that smell damp. Make sure any inspector you hire has this information.

### AIR-CONDITIONING CONDENSERS AND TRASH CANS

Air-conditioning units and trash cans, as much as we depend on them, aren't going to win any beauty contests. They tend to give a ratty look to their immediate surroundings as well. Lay down some river rocks in these areas; this is a big improvement over bare dirt, dead grass, and weeds. Wipe down condensers and trash cans, and keep only your best-looking cans. In staging, even your trash is clean. If the cans are tidy and lined up, if their placement seems purposeful, then you're okay. If you have the time and money in your budget, camouflage them behind bushes or attractive fencing. If you're handy and can dig a few post holes, you can put up lattice fencing relatively inexpensively.

### DRIVEWAYS AND WALKWAYS

Check the state of your driveway. Patch or reseal it if it's cracked. Sealing it is a full day's project; some sellers hire a professional for this work and

**Figure 4–3.** Before: *This driveway is merely functional, adding little to the exterior look of the home. The plantings dwarf the house and hide the door, and the transition between the hardtop and the lawn and pathway is too abrupt.*

some do it themselves. If you have a gravel or unfinished driveway area, it probably needs to be leveled. You'll find it easier to add dirt or gravel to the ruts and other low spots than to shave down the high spots. If you raise the bed of the driveway by adding dirt, it will be more likely to drain water away—always a good thing. Then add fresh stones to the driveway over the dirt. Not being a weight lifter, this is something that I outsource, but if you feel able, go for it. A well maintained driveway is a crucial aspect of curb appeal. To me, it's the difference between a freshly starched and ironed shirt, and one that is wrinkled.

While we're thinking about cars, if you have a garage with a door, make sure the door works easily, whether it's automatic or not.

Your walkways need to be in great shape, with no surprises for the unwary foot. It's such a downer when a prospective buyer twists an ankle on the way into your home. If your walkways are broken or sunken, relay them or hire someone to do this. If you have a concrete path, you can greatly enhance the curb appeal of your property by removing it and replacing it with bricks or stones. I admit that this process is labor intensive, but it will make a huge difference.

*Figure 4–4.* **After:** *Plants in pots help to soften the transition between the driveway and the lawn, and pruning the existing shrubs opens up the full view of the house.*

*Laying a New Path*

*Pull up your pavers or brick if you have a loose path. Chisel out cement if the path is cement. Dig a trench the size of the path about six inches deep. Lay down about two inches of what is called crusher—a mix of coarse pebbles and concrete that improves drainage. Next add concrete sand, which will hold your pavers or bricks better than regular sand and further enhance drainage. When you pour the concrete sand, use a level to be sure that the sand is level or evenly canted at the same grade. This makes it much easier to align the stones or bricks. Then, lay your bricks or pavers on top, placing them closely and carefully. Finally, pour some more concrete sand over the top and sweep it so that it fills in any cracks between the paving bricks or stones.*

### DECKS, TERRACES, AND FENCES

Check all decks, terraces, and fences for rot, water damage, termites, and soundness. Have them replaced if they're broken or aging. These structures are often among the first things prospective buyers see when entering your property, and they directly affect curb appeal. If I see a broken fence, I immediately suspect—and usually rightly so—that the home's interior also needs a fair amount of work.

If you have a wooden deck, resealing it will be well worth your time. This is not a hard job: Sweep or brush the deck, then use a roller and roll on deck sealer. Ta-da! Your deck has a fresh look without a lot of effort. Make sure that all railings and banisters are sound (check those inside your home too). When a buyer takes hold of any part of your property, you want it to feel solid.

### WINDOWS FROM THE OUTSIDE

Replace any broken window panes and screens. If you can't do this yourself, you can usually hire a handy person to do it very inexpensively. Screens, especially older screens, block out a lot of light. If they're not being used when the property goes on the market, take them out, label them carefully as to which room and which window they go in, and store them. If you have shutters, make sure that they're clean and in good repair.

### EXTERIOR WALL AND TRIM PAINT

Check all exterior wall and trim paint. Sand and repaint any peeling paint. Not only does peeling paint announce that the house is not in pristine condition, but it also makes prospective buyers worry that the wall or trim underneath is damp and rotting. Remember, paint started as a way to provide protection from the elements. We all—including your potential buyers—have a primordial wish to keep the elements out so that we feel protected in our living space.

If your exterior paint is in terrible shape in general, consider repainting the house. Of course, painting a house is not cheap, particularly if you hire a really good painting company. Here's what we did with one client to keep costs down: Faced with staging a huge old house that needed much remedial and aesthetic work, we hired painters to paint the exterior trim only on the front of the house. This highlighted the sweet Victorian detailing in the architecture, and when prospective buyers entered the covered front porch, they got a sense of how the property could be if they brought it back to its original glory. Now, let's see what the inside of your home needs in the way of repairs.

---

### The Staging Survival Kit: Our Favorite Cleaning Aids

*Here are some fabulous products that we cannot be without. Give them a try; they make a huge difference.*

❖ **Goo Gone.** *Use it to remove marker, dirt, and unidentifiable caked-on stuff. It is amazing, but strong, although not as strong as its harsher, more powerful cousin Goof Off.*

❖ **Magic Eraser.** *I no longer believe in the tooth fairy, but I have yet to be disillusioned by this wonderful tool. It takes away shoe marks, crayon,* *marker, scuffs, and scrapes. We use it on stair risers and walls every day. We only wish that it worked on cars. Test it on a small area of paint first because it will occasionally discolor flat paint finishes, especially older ones.*

❖ ***Wood markers.*** *Get a variety of colors. They cover a multitude of scratches and blemishes. Remember that buyers are judging you on how you treat all of your belongings, not just your home. If your dining room table has a gash in it, buyers will make the subconscious leap that your home has a metaphoric gash in it too.*

❖ ***Bleach pen.*** *Use this to clean grout or any other hard-to-get-at spot; it's very satisfying and much cheaper than therapy.*

❖ ***Minwax Hardwood Floor Reviver.*** *Use this to refinish your floors beautifully. At about $18 a bottle, it is pricey compared to other floor pol-ishes, but cheap compared to a professional refinishing job. I recently did my bedroom floor, and I can't believe the difference.*

❖ ***Chandelier cleaner spray.*** *This will save you from having to clean each crystal by hand. Simply place a towel below your chandelier, spray on the cleaner, and watch the dirt and grime drip off. Any number of brands work well.*

## INTERIOR WALLS AND CEILINGS

Check the ceiling and walls in every room. If you see any mold, mildew, cracks, or water damage, you need to address these issues. Buyers are partic-ularly wary of water damage because it conjures up all kinds of scary thoughts about a shelter not really sheltering, and money flying out the damp crack. Saying, "Oh, but we fixed that crack," will not cut it, even if you did fix it. Fix the *reminder* of the leak as well as the leak itself, or you might as well have water pouring into your home. A leak that is truly dry usually needs just one coat of paint; at most, you'll need to sand and then paint.

Buy some paint grade (100- to 150-grit) sandpaper, and sand every crack or imperfection in your paint. You are going to need a paint sample from each wall, so grab a chip before you sand. A chip about the size of a half-dollar is big enough. Even if you have leftover paint, if it isn't new, it has probably changed color while on the wall. Take the chip to any paint or hardware store. They should be able to match it electronically.

Buy spackle. Spackling is easy and even enjoyable. Using a spackling knife, spread spackle over the cracks like butter, trying to smooth it down so that there are no ridges. Let it dry for a day and then sand lightly with very fine sandpaper. If your cracks are too big to spackle, you will need to buy mesh tape or even crack patches. Paint salespeople love to help you through this process, so enlist their assistance. Spackling, sanding, and painting do not constitute hard work and must be done.

Even in college, I enjoyed the occasional do-it-yourself project. I probably should not admit that at the end of each year, we would patch the holes in our walls with toothpaste so that we wouldn't get fined for damage! Please don't use toothpaste as spackle when staging your home.

If mildew is an issue, wipe the area down with a mix of one cup of borax per quart of water (see also the section on basements, attics, garages, and outbuildings, "Clean Is What Sells"), and then let it dry for a day. You may need to use a product like Kilz, which is a sealer for mildew and tobacco stains. You treat it like a primer and then paint over it. (There are other such products, but Kilz is our favorite. See "Kilz: A Miraculous Product.")

Most homeowners have a few walls that have taken a real beating because of all the pictures that have been hung on them. My advice is to spackle and repaint the whole wall in these cases. If you haven't already done so when reading Chapter Three, this is the moment to remove all three-dimensional wall art. It eats into the space in a room and is almost always too taste specific. I am using the term "art" loosely. I mean, remove hanging sculptures, quilts, moose heads, anything that extends outward from the wall. You will probably have to remove large nails or screws and then spackle, sand, and paint over the holes.

I hate beige switch plates. Whoever invented them deserves a special seat in aesthetic purgatory, in my view. Go through your property and review your switch plates. If they are white, chrome, or even brass (preferably old brass), they are okay and probably just need a good wipe-down. If they are another color—beige, wallpapered, who knows what some crafty soul might have come up with—remove them and buy white ones. They usually cost less than a dollar and can be screwed in and out very easily.

---

### Kilz: A Miraculous Product

*We use Kilz primer wherever we encounter any sort of problem surface. I discovered it about fifteen years ago when we bought a house owned by a chain-smoker. We'd hired a firm to paint the interior. Within a month, tobacco resin was seeping in large golden drops through our fresh ceiling paint. You can imagine how I felt about this. We wiped the ceilings down, stripped them as best we could, and then discovered Kilz. It can be used on almost all interior surfaces and covers smoke damage; stops wood resin and knots from bleeding through; covers water stains; blocks pet smells, mold, and mildew; and can be used to seal wallpaper for a quick fix if you want to paint over it without taking the trouble to strip it. Kilz comes in different types for different surfaces and uses; some types are stronger than others and may require more ventilation as you work. If you're not clear on which type to buy, ask a paint salesperson. This is a miraculous product.*

---

#### OVERHEAD LIGHTING AND CEILING FANS

I am not a big fan of overhead light fixtures, unless they are recessed. These fixtures intrude into a room, making it seem dated and smaller. Very often they've been retrofitted with ceiling fans that remind buyers that you don't have central air conditioning. Cap overhead fixtures if possible, unless an overhead light serves an immediate purpose (such as lighting a dining room or kitchen table or a pool table) or extends down out of a historic plaster medallion and fits the period of the room. In most cases, capping an overhead fixture improves the look of a room.

I don't recommend fiddling with the electrical system yourself unless you really know what you're doing. If not, hire an electrician who's insured.

### WINDOWS FROM THE INSIDE

First, make sure that all your sash hinges work and match. It's easy to unscrew these and replace them. Next, make sure that any window latches and locks work well and look good. Replace any that are dated, pitted, or broken. You can do this yourself. Buy nice looking white or brass fixtures and perhaps stainless ones for the bathrooms and kitchen.

If you have old sash windows, they may not even line up correctly anymore, so that the window latches can't do their job. Fix as many of these problems as you can; if the job proves too tricky, hire someone if you can afford it.

If your sash windows don't open easily, try spraying their tracks with cooking spray. Very often, windows in older homes have been painted shut. Unsealing them is tricky and usually requires repainting. For staging purposes, it probably is not worth the time and effort to unseal them. Let's leave the new owners something to do (but remember to let them know about this problem up front).

Windowsills in particular really take a beating. We often go over every sill with a quick coat of semigloss or high gloss paint (sanding out any cracked or peeling areas first). The new paint not only makes everything seem fresh, but also easily blends into the room as a whole because the new paint meets the old at a sharply defined edge. Use the paint that matches the rest of the window trim, if you can get it; if not, you can use a good, clean white like Benjamin Moore's 925 that will go well with almost any color. At the very least, walk around with the appropriate paint can and fill in any chips or nicks you find on windowsills.

### How to Paint Patches

*When you're painting over a relatively small patch of wall, ceiling, or other painted surface, feather out the edges of the new paint with light, lifting strokes. To cover the area, you may need to repeat this process. Your results may not be perfect, but remember that this is painting for staging, not for a new professional career for you.*

**Figure 4–5.** *Before: Gaps like this one are common but not reassuring to prospective buyers. This one is especially disturbing because of its location on a stair landing. Buyers will see it at eye level, perhaps not even registering it consciously, but noting it all the same.*

Finally, if you can bring yourself to do it, *please* remove any window-mounted air-conditioning units. These units hurt your staging efforts in so many ways: They're always dirty and never attractive, they announce loudly to prospective buyers that you don't have central air conditioning, and they block natural light. Enough said; they're an anti-staging hat trick.

### STAIRCASES

Stairs endure a lot of traffic. Remove all wall-to-wall carpeting from them. You can replace the carpeting if you wish, but I can assure you that it needs to come up. Wax the treads and paint the risers with your semigloss trim paint. I would hazard a guess that in at least half of all homes with more than one storey, the main stairway faces the front door. In these cases, the stairs are front and center in prospective buyers' first impressions. I have yet to see an unremediated set that look good.

If you need to replace the runner on a staircase, don't let the installers use the waterfall method of installing the rug; they prefer it because it's easier to do, but it catches dirt in the gap between the tread and the riser. Ask them to install contour carpeting.

Sometimes along the bottom of a baseboard, especially on stairs (perhaps because of settling), there are unsightly gaps. Cover these gaps (along the entire baseboard or staircase, not just where a gap is) with what is called quarter-round.

### WALL-TO-WALL CARPETING

Used wall-to-wall carpeting—meaning anyone else's—is so unappealing that it can kill a sale. For prospective buyers, it conjures up visions of allergies and cat urine. In truth, when people live with their wall-to-wall carpeting for a while,

they stop seeing the stains and they don't necessarily notice if it begins to smell.

I've already suggested that you remove all wall-to-wall carpeting from stairs. In fact, I recommend removing any wall-to-wall carpeting that you can, particularly if you have a pet (in which case you must remove it) or if the carpeting is more than three years old. If the stairs or flooring underneath are in terrible

Figure 4–6. After: With new, painted quarter-round covering the gap along the edge of the stairs, prospective buyers won't even notice this part of your home—which is as it should be. The property seems solid and airtight.

*Figure 4–7. Before: The tiling around the toilet is worn and cracking.*

shape or aren't hardwood, install new carpeting. A neutral, tight weave carpet is a good choice on stairs.

When replacing carpets, don't trust your own taste. Remember, staging is about removing your taste to make room for prospective buyers' dreams. Ask the rug installers what is the best-selling neutral carpet and install that. Avoid any patterns or trims on rugs; they make rooms seem smaller, and patterns will turn off some buyers.

### Replacing Transition Strips

*What's a transition strip? It's that piece of chrome or cheesy brass (usually) that's tacked on the threshold between rooms with different carpets or where carpet changes to hardwood. For $10 to $20 apiece, you can buy wooden transition strips to replace cheap metal ones. These will improve the look of your rooms significantly.*

We recently staged a home valued at over a million dollars. Its great room was covered in wall-to-wall baby blue carpeting, and its dining room and living room featured desert brown shag. Unless this home was going to be made into a living history museum of bourgeois American material culture circa 1980, this carpeting had to be replaced. When we were hired, the home had been on the market for six months without a bid. After changing the carpet, it sold within a month.

Replacing carpets should be done professionally. Depending on your area, you'll pay about $10 per square yard to have new wall-to-wall carpeting installed. New and cheap is better than old and grungy.

### FLOORING

Often we find old linoleum or vinyl flooring in kitchens and bathrooms. Few things are more depressing to me than a deteriorating linoleum or vinyl floor, stained and cracked, with a few squares gnawed along the edges by some ill-mannered house pet that died in 1973. An easy way to update the look

*Figure 4–8.* **After: With new tiling in place, the bathroom is rejuvenated, and the floor now appears reassuringly watertight to prospective buyers. Notice also that we painted the sink water pipes white to minimize their effect.**

of a kitchen without breaking the bank is to overlay cork, vinyl, or linoleum tiles (you should be able to find them for under $4 each) on the existing tiles. Before you do this, remove any damaged tiles and replace them with new ones. These don't need to match the color; the purpose is just to create an even underflooring. Ecologically green cork tiling costs anywhere from $1 to $4 per square foot. The kind of vinyl flooring that you roll out and cut to fit the room is cheap but can be difficult to use.

Figure 4–9. Before: The interior of this front door has several problems: The paint is chipped and dirty; the threshold plate is cheap looking; and there are gaps between the floorboards and the wall.

### DOORS AND DOORWAYS

Doors also come in for a lot of rough treatment. Check doors and their frames with that can of paint in your hand (paint that matches the door trim, of course), and dab over any nicks or cuts in the paint. One way to give your home an inexpensive makeover is to replace the doorknobs. In many homes I visit, the doorknobs are cheap and have become pitted and unattractive with age. Frequently, every door has a different style of knob. Most people won't consciously notice this, but poor, mismatched doorknobs do detract from the appeal of a home.

This is something that you can do yourself. To start, take off the old knob, noting which side of the door it's on, and bring it to the hardware store. Here's the tricky part: you need to install the new lock (if any) and doorknob so that they work properly on the side of the door opposite from the hinge. This requirement is difficult to explain in words and inevitably creates a number of those who's-on-first moments at the hardware store. (I find that drawing pictures and using pantomime can prevent frustrating results back home.) Then follow the instructions for installation.

If this seems daunting, hire someone to install the new knobs. You'll be amazed at how much your new doorknobs, both interior and exterior, will transform your home. Prospective buyers will go through all the doors in your home. You want the doorknobs to feel substantial.

## KITCHENS

Kitchen drawers should slide easily, and nothing should fall on you when you open any cabinet doors. All drawers work differently, so you may need to do some forensic investigation. Spritzing some cooking spray or

Figure 4–10. After: With fresh paint, a nicer threshold plate, new quarter-round covering the gaps, and a new brass doorknob that feels substantial when held, the situation is greatly improved.

*Figure 4–11.* **Before:** *This bathroom sink is old. Its sealant is cracking and dirty, the medicine cabinet and shelf are dated, and too much of the owner's presence remains visible on the shelf.*

WD-40 onto the gears or wooden slides often works wonders. Review Chapter Three if your cabinets are still so full that things are toppling out when you open them.

We often use Kilz to help us update kitchen cabinetry. After wiping out all the kitchen cabinets, paint them inside and out with two coats of Kilz primer, and then paint the outside of the cabinets with a high gloss light-colored enamel. You can paint the insides of drawers and cabinetry with a medium-toned semigloss (see Chapter Six for advice on using color) or line them with fresh, neutral contact paper. Stained drawer liners are quite unattractive and so easy to fix.

Buy new knobs and handles in brushed chrome. What a difference! This is also the time to order any missing knobs or other parts for appliances.

*Figure 4–12.* **After: *Replacing the sink, the cabinet, and the shelf has given this bathroom a complete facelift. The finishing touch was to remove the too-personal items.***

They usually come in ten days from the manufacturer. Have a contractor remove the old laminate countertop and replace it with some of the new and very hip laminates—some of which I prefer to stone—and you have a new kitchen.

### BATHROOMS

You can easily update the look of your bathroom simply by replacing the medicine cabinet. If it's an inside mount or electrified, you probably need to get professional help, but if you're a confident do-it-yourselfer, have at it! Don't forget to cover your sink with several towels to protect it; breaking one fixture while trying to replace another is awfully frustrating.

New toilet seats are a must, especially on old toilets. You can unscrew these yourself, but be sure to measure your old toilet seats because you'll find several sizes to choose from at the supply store. Get white seats. Even if a toilet is another color, unless its seat is pristine—and I mean perfect—I replace the seat with a white one. It just seems fresher. I'm not a big fan of wooden toilet seats, but they are another option if your toilets aren't white and you can't get an exact color match. For about $500 you can have the entire toilet replaced, which is preferable and well worth the money if you can afford it. Replacing bathroom fixtures is a great way to rehab a bathroom. New bathrooms make sales and boost prices.

Latex caulk often peels off, and leaves an opportunity for mildew and leaking. If the seal is broken, pull out all latex caulking around a sink or tub. Tape the edges so that you have a narrow strip of open space where you want the caulk to go, then squirt it into the space using a caulk gun. Wait a day before removing the tape. You can also buy caulking tape that you press into the gap; some people find this easier to use than a caulk gun.

Make sure all your sink and tub faucets work, that the handles are in good shape (order replacements if they're chipped, broken, or rusted), and that your bathtub and shower drain properly. Buyers will often turn on faucets, so fix these problems yourself if you can or hire a plumber if you can't.

This brings us to the end of the repair section. Now that you've fixed whatever you can fix, it's time to clean your home from top to bottom.

## Clean Is What Sells

Before you put your property on the market, you should clean it with a vengeance. Depending on how much time and money you have, you can do this yourself, invite a bunch of family and friends to help you (just the neatnik ones—you know who they are; see "Throw a Cleaning, Gardening, or Painting Party"), or hire a housecleaner, maybe even a professional team for a deep cleaning. Either way, this endeavor must be head and shoulders above the average weekly cleaning; you're going for the spring cleaning they write about in Victorian novels, except that you won't have to boil great tubs of water on a coal-fired stove.

Some general advice about cleaning is to look up! I've noticed that people tend to clean only as far up as they can see or easily reach. I am tall, and my husband is very tall. We see a lot of grunge on top shelves and on the tops of fridges, cabinets, cornices, and lighting fixtures. Look down, too, and under things—anywhere that you don't normally inspect. Also, when you're cleaning, work from the top down or you'll find yourself having to clean the lower parts all over again when the grime from higher up succumbs to gravity.

Start with the outside of your property—where buyers will form their first impressions—and work your way in. Once you're inside, you may want to start with the bathrooms and kitchen first, as they are such hot spots for dirt. And finally, as you wash walls and weed your walkways, think of the dollars you're adding to your curb appeal.

Now, as for particular advice, beginning with the outdoors, the following sections take you through a thorough cleaning process.

### Throw a Cleaning, Gardening, or Painting Party

*Getting a home ready for sale can be daunting. Consider enlisting the help of friends and family. So often, people want to help in some way during life transitions and don't know how. Tell them that you really don't need a casserole; what you need is elbow grease. Ask them to help. Beg and plead and make it fun.*

*When we moved into our new house, we needed to put up fencing for our dogs. We had pretty much maxed out our cash on hand and were terrified that the dogs would get hit by a car. A friend suggested that people like to pitch in and that we should buy fence supplies, pizza, and beer, and invite all our friends over for a fence-raising party. In the end, we opted for a fence dug professionally and a payment plan, but her essential idea was a good one. Have your friends over—either during the day for coffee, Danish, and cleaning (or gardening work, or painting, or moving furniture—whatever you need most) or during the evening. Serve chili or pizza, and then hand out the assignments. If you're cleaning, assign each person a task, not a room. Someone cleans all the grout, another washes walls, and so on. Make sure you have plenty of supplies on hand for whatever work you're doing.*

*If asking family or friends to help you clean feels uncomfortable, find a couple of friends who also need cleaning help and create a cleaning co-op. Start with your property so that you can get it on the market, and then move on to their homes (you'll need to be out of your home anyway during showings). You can ask your realtor if he or she knows about others who would be moving at about the same time and who might be interested in this idea.*

### YARDS AND GARDENS

Review Chapter Two for specific advice on making your yard and gardens look their best. Be sure to maintain them regularly while your home is on the market. "Clean," for outdoor areas, means no weeds or leaves in paths, lawns, or gardens. It means a sense of orderliness, with cleanly edged garden beds, for example. If you have a pool, it should be open and pristine.

### ROOFS AND EXTERIOR WALLS

Have your roofs swept and gutters cleaned before you go any further. If you are brave and can handle this safely, do it yourself. I am afraid of heights, so I hire professionals for this job.

If there is mildew on your roof or walls, you need to remove it. Review the section about interior walls and ceilings under "Commonly Needed Repairs," and see also the section about basements, attics, garages, and outbuildings. These sections describe the proper mix of borax and water for attacking mildew and mold. You may want to call in the pros to power wash the exterior walls with an antifungal liquid. Some stains on walls may require a coat of paint. Remember, your home's exterior doesn't need to be stripped and painted perfectly for staging purposes.

Have the house power washed, if possible, perhaps while you're having the windows cleaned (see "Windows"). You might be surprised at how much better your home looks without all those cobwebs under the eaves. If you have a terrace or porch, have that power washed too. If you live in a sandy or dusty area, you may need to have your home power washed more than once while it's on the market.

## WINDOWS

Get your windows professionally cleaned. Do not scrimp on this detail. It's almost as important as uncluttering. Compared to packing up your high school football plays, hiring a window washer is pretty easy and will cost $200 to $500 for the average home. Many people skip this step, not wanting to spend the money and thinking—quite wrongly—that people won't notice the windows. Your buyers may not be able to verbalize what feels good about your windows, but they certainly will notice. Clean windows let in much more light. Windows are big selling points, so don't neglect them. The largest bill I ever got for window cleaning was $1,900—and that was for a 12,000-square-foot home. Your realtor probably knows of a good window washer; otherwise, find someone who had this job done and was happy with the results.

Have storm windows and screens cleaned as well, if applicable and possible. If the weather is too cold for screens or if you've removed them to let more light into your home, label them carefully so that the new owner has no doubt about which screen goes into which window.

In the same vein, please remove any sheer curtains or internal shutters that block light. Clean venetian blinds thoroughly (that is, if you want to keep them at all), and pull them all the way up. Even in their open positions, these window treatments make rooms feel smaller.

## INTERIOR WALLS AND CEILINGS

Wipe down all walls, baseboards, and crown moldings. Get those cobwebs lurking in the high corners and the odd strand of web hanging down from your ceilings. Force yourself to apply a rag or duster to every surface. You'll be surprised at what you find. On any painted surface, the Magic

Eraser will be your new best friend (see "The Staging Survival Kit: Our Favorite Cleaning Aids").

### OVERHEAD LIGHTING AND CEILING FANS

Clean and repair all ceiling lights. If you refuse to remove your ceiling fans, wipe them down. They gather lots of dust. They should at least be clean eyesores. I often replace fan blades as a matter of course; sometimes that's easier than cleaning them. If you have glass or crystal chandeliers, use chandelier cleaner spray (see "The Staging Survival Kit: Our Favorite Cleaning Aids").

### FLOORS AND CARPETS

Clean and polish all the floors. Wash them with lemon or vinegar and water, or Murphy's Oil Soap and water. For any wax, grease, or material that won't come off, use Goof Off, which is very strong. Try a bit in an inconspicuous area to make sure it doesn't remove your finish or paint. Goo Gone is its much kinder, gentler cousin. Although Goo Gone is good for sensitive surfaces, I love the power of Goof Off. On wood floors, after cleaning them, use Minwax Hardwood Floor Reviver. (See "The Staging Survival Kit: Our Favorite Cleaning Aids").

In the same spirit, have all your carpets cleaned. Any area rugs that will be in your home while it's being shown should be professionally cleaned. If you aren't going to have them cleaned, remove them. The same thing goes for wall-to-wall carpeting, which is discussed at length under "Commonly Needed Repairs."

### KITCHENS

Clean, clean, clean, and put away. All those objects and appliances that you think you need on the counter—make them go away. Command central for most people, kitchens are hot spots of clutter and mess. Review Chapter Three if you still have too much stuff on your counters and in your cabinets.

Clean all appliances inside and out, whether or not you're selling them with the property. Your buyers are judging you on your ability to maintain a home, and cleanliness adds value. Clean all shelves, drawers, and cabinets, inside and out. When you've emptied them, that's a good time to separate the things you really use from those you really don't want to pay to move. Wipe down all your counters, cabinets, and pulls. You don't want potential buyers to try to open a drawer, only to find it sticky from your child's recent foray after lunch.

Clean the inside and outside of your ovens and refrigerator. These must look as pristine as possible. A paste of baking soda and water, spread all over the interior of your oven and left overnight, makes a good nontoxic oven cleaner if your oven doesn't have a self-cleaning setting. Just wipe it off in the morning. Don't forget to clean the top, sides, and back of your fridge, and whatever little shop of horrors you find underneath it when you pull it (carefully!) away from the wall. Clean under your stove too, if you can, and do read the following cautions about cleaning up after rodents.

### Cleaning Up After Rodents Safely

*If you find evidence of mice inside your home or in an outbuilding, be extremely careful when cleaning up their leavings. Certain types of mice and rats transmit something called hantavirus pulmonary syndrome (HPS), a potentially deadly disease that we can contract through fresh mouse urine, droppings, or saliva, or—if you stir up contaminated areas—through the air. According to the Centers for Disease Control and Prevention (CDC), common house mice don't carry HPS, but deer mice, white-footed mice, rice rats, and cotton rats do. At least one of these rodent types probably lives in your part of the country.*

*You may decide to call in the pros if you have a lot of rodent debris to remove. If you're cleaning up after rodents yourself, the main precaution to bear in mind is that you don't want to touch, stir up, or breathe in particles of their leavings. To avoid doing these things, says the CDC, wear rubber gloves while you clean, and spray down the leavings with a disinfectant (a 10 percent bleach solution works well, but most household cleaners will also do the job) to both deactivate the virus and dampen the leavings so that they won't become airborne. Clean up the urine and droppings carefully, bagging them tightly. If you happen upon any dead rodents, bag them while wearing gloves and dispose of them. After you've gotten rid of any such delights, disinfect anything (including your gloves, while they're still on your hands) that might have been contaminated. Finally, remove your gloves, dispose of them as well, and wash your hands thoroughly with soap and water.*

*Some hantavirus strains are quite deadly, some aren't, and it's rare that people contract this disease. But there's no cure for it yet. Why risk it? Take the precautions.*

### BATHROOMS

Bathrooms take a beating in every home. Replace your shower curtains and use a bleach pen on all grout. Clean every nook and cranny of your toilets. Dust off the tops and shades of any light fixtures on the walls. Dust the tops of towel racks, toilet paper holders, baseboards, mirrors—any surface that can hold dust. Reach up with the vacuum cleaner extension and clean off the ceiling exhaust fan. Clean toothpaste sprinklings off your mirrors daily. Clean hair out from sinks and around shower and tub drains daily. Wash the floors regularly and make sure any bathmat is clean, dry, and off the floor during showings. Wipe out every drawer and cabinet. Hide medicines and prescription drugs. In staging, no one gets sick, and it is nobody's business what medicines you take.

### LAUNDRY ROOMS

Ironically, laundry rooms are often filthy. They attract dust and lint. Wipe down the washer and dryer inside and out, including the area around the dryer vent. This is also a good time to clean out any lint buildup in the dryer vent, which is a horrible fire hazard. Clean around the vent where it exits your home as well; this is usually an unsightly area.

**FIREPLACES, RADIATORS, AND OTHER HEAT-RELATED OBJECTS**

Fireplaces usually need attention. Clean out the hearth: Brush it out carefully and wipe it down. Polish your andirons and lay the fire. We use birch logs if we can find them, because they tend to lighten an area that is a visual black hole in so many homes. Dried hydrangea can also lighten the hearth.

If you have a woodstove, clean it out thoroughly, including any glass doors. GoJo works well to remove soot from woodstove doors; so does a single-edge razor blade if you're careful with it. Clean and polish the outside with appropriate agents (ask either the company that sold you the stove, if possible, or a chimney sweep).

Homeowners often don't notice that their heating and cooling registers and radiators have attracted a lot of dust and grime. Take them off, wash them, and, if necessary, give them a fresh coat of the appropriate type of paint (for example, use radiator paint only on radiators). Paint them the same colors as the walls or ceiling they are attached to. Don't paint them the trim color: This draws too much attention to them.

Remember not to use chemicals on anything that gets hot! If you do, you'll be breathing in those fumes the next time you light a fire. This goes for electric baseboard heating too: Vacuum these heaters and then wipe down with dishwashing soap and water.

**BASEMENTS, ATTICS, GARAGES, AND OUTBUILDINGS**

You'd be wise to wear a mask before attempting to clean out these notoriously filthy areas; much of what you'll disturb while cleaning them is not safe to breathe. Also, since they may be damp as well as dirty from long neglect, you should buy, borrow, or rent a wet-dry shop vacuum rather than overtaxing your regular vacuum cleaner or risking a shock.

Clean your basements, attics, garages, and outbuildings as if they were rooms in the main part of your home. (You've already uncluttered them, right? If not, review Chapter Three and do that first.) Remove all dust and spiderwebs from duct work and piping. Storm doors and outside steps to basements are magnets for seasonal debris. Make sure that you sweep or blow them out. Sweep out garages and vacuum attics, if possible. Look vigilantly for signs of mice or other rodents (see "Cleaning Up after Rodents Safely," which you should read before tackling any mouse droppings), and check also for mold. If you think there's any chance that you have black mold, *call in a professional.* Black mold can be lethal.

### Safety Guidelines for Cleaning Up Mold

*Before cleaning up moldy situations, follow these safety guidelines:*

❖ *Seal the area in which you'll be cleaning up the mold. This is especially crucial in the basement, where I want you to close all vents and heating and air-conditioning ducts that open up to other rooms besides the mold-affected room.*

❖ *Keep doors and windows to the outside open.*

❖ *Wear work goggles, rubber gloves, a long-sleeved shirt, and pants, as well as an OSHA-approved dust mask. Mold is irritating at best and dangerous at worst.*

❖ *Contrary to conventional wisdom, bleach does not kill mold at its core. Borax is preferable. To clean mold, mix one cup of borax per quart of hot water in a clean bucket. Scrub down the moldy area using a stiff scrub brush.*

❖ *Don't rinse the walls after scrubbing. Allow the borax solution to dry on the walls, and then vacuum up the residue the next day. If you have a major mold issue, rent a Concrobium Mold Control Fogger ($25 a day at a home supply store), which atomizes a mold-fighting solution so that you can easily mist large surfaces as well as difficult-to-reach places. The Fogger will cover up to a 20 × 20 foot (1,500 square foot) room in thirty minutes.*

Once your basement is clean, you might want to whitewash the walls for a fresh look. You probably don't need to parget the walls for staging purposes. If anything, I would apply Kilz in white instead of regular paint.

## If Time and Money Are Short

I cannot tell you the number of times that I've gotten a call asking if I can stage a home this week—"We have an open house on Saturday!" Life takes surprising turns, and suddenly you are packing for a new job that starts in two weeks across the country. Life is expensive too. You probably bought this book because hiring a professional stager is not in the financial cards right now. So, with time and money in short supply, what are the top priorities in repairing and cleaning your home?

---

### Must-Do List for Fixing and Cleaning

*Remember, in my experience, any money that owners spend during the staging process comes back to them, **and then some**, when they sell their home. Whether you're short on time, money, or both, here's what you must do:*

❖ *Fix anything that's broken or doesn't function correctly. If you don't have time to fix it yourself, hire someone to do it. You will pay less now to have it fixed than you will in a lowered sales price or in the concessions that you make at closing.*

❖ *Get a professional estimate on repair costs for any large issues you're aware of.*

❖ *Fix leaky faucets.*

❖ *Prune your shrubs away from windows and pathways.*

❖ *Have your yard and garden weeded, edged, mulched, and mowed.*

❖ *Get your windows cleaned.*

❖ *Replace any switch plates that aren't white, chrome, or brass.*

❖ *Pull up wall-to-wall carpeting if you own a pet. Either replace it with new carpeting or refinish the floor underneath it.*

❖ *Clean your home from top to bottom.*

❖ *Clean your appliances inside and out.*

❖ *Bleach your grout.*

## THE NEXT STEP: SETTING THE STAGE

Now that your home is uncluttered, repaired, and cleaned, you've probably decided that you don't really want to sell it after all! But just in case you still do, get ready for the fun part of staging, when you carefully arrange that dream home for your prospective buyers. In Chapter Five, you'll learn how to use furnishings, accessories, color, and style to create a sense of flow, focus, and balance in all parts of your home.

C H A P T E R 5

# Setting
# the Stage

*Buildings are the books that every body [sic] unconsciously reads.*
—*Charles B. Fairbanks*, My Unknown Chum

**WELL, YOU'VE** done the hard work.

- ❖ You've identified your likely target market and said good-bye to your home (Chapter One).

- ❖ You've taken most of the things out of your home that made it truly your own (Chapter Three).

- ❖ You've repaired things that needed repairing as best you could (Chapter Four).

❖ You've cleaned your home right down to the frame (also Chapter Four).

❖ You've even transformed the entrance to your home into a more inviting prospect for potential buyers (Chapter Two).

Your home probably feels strange and empty, although you may be greatly enjoying the space you've created in it, how well everything works,

*Figure 5–1.* **Before:** *Having the sideboard in this dining room has forced the table to sit too far over to be directly under the overhead light fixture, which throws the room off balance.*

and how clean it is. But now it's time for the fun stuff: setting the stage of your home so that it appeals immensely to your most likely buyers.

Using the analogy of your entire home as a theater stage (and each room as a mini stage), think of yourself as the set designer. Your job is to choose and arrange the furnishings, accessories, backdrops, lighting, and color that support your goal: enticing your most likely buyers to see themselves living happily within this space you've created. Or think of yourself

*Figure 5–2.* **After: With the sideboard removed, the dining room table is centered under the light fixture, as it should be.**

as a marketing executive. Your product is your home, and your market is whatever generational group is most likely to buy that product. Every choice you make in preparing your home for sale should support your branding of your property. You must keep asking yourself, "Will *this* [wall color, window treatment, armchair, knickknack, or whatever] appeal to my most likely group of buyers?"

When I'm staging a home, I bring in furniture, rugs, accessories, paintings, plants, and so on to appeal specifically to a target market. Read my tips in this chapter and review those in Chapter One (see "Understanding the Generations") and Chapter Two ("Impressing Your Target Buyer") for what does and does not appeal to various generations, and look at your possessions with fresh eyes to see what you have on hand that will suit. You may or may not have the resources to buy, rent, or borrow things from outside; this is fine if you can use what you have in a creative, purposeful way. You may also bring in some new things to enhance your home for potential buyers. The things you choose to place in your home during the selling process do *not* need to match your property stylistically; they need to match the needs and desires of prospective buyers. And each room must work in concert with every other room to create a cohesive message that helps that mysterious, ultimate buyer to fall in love with your home.

## DECIDING EACH ROOM'S PURPOSE

First, you'll need to figure out exactly how each room will be used during the selling process. Maybe you're thinking, "But they already have obvious uses! The kitchen . . . the dining room . . . the bedrooms . . . what else could they be?" Consider this: People crave balance in their lives. A balanced life includes work, eating, sleeping, bathing, leisure time, solitude, and exercise. When prospective buyers view a home, they want to imagine themselves living in that home and leading The Balanced Life that they long for, not the nitty-gritty reality. At the very least, they'll need a kitchen, a bedroom or two (depending on family size), some kind of communal room, and at least one bathroom, but they'll want more. People want space for all the facets of their lives. Depending on their generation, they'll want somewhat different types of rooms in their ideal home.

### TARGETING ROOM USAGE TO YOUR MOST LIKELY BUYERS

Take a moment to go back to Chapter One. Review the lists of what each generation wants (see "Understanding the Generations"). As you look over the list of what your most likely buyers will want, mentally tour your home. If your target market is a young family, you may want to recast a grown-up's bedroom as a children's bedroom and, if you have enough space, to set up one room on the first floor as a playroom. You can also create a grown-ups' playroom aimed at your target generation. For Gen Xers and Gen Yers, a media room almost always trumps a library. Boomers like a librarylike office, and Jonesers are fighting their forty-something bodies with a workout room. You don't need to import fancy equipment for this: If you have a small, empty room, throw down a yoga mat and brightly colored exercise ball, and add a basket with rolled-up spa towels and bottled water. Don't sacrifice a bedroom for any of these unless you have plenty of bedrooms already.

> ### When You Should Keep a Bedroom as a Bedroom
> *Unless you have four or more bedrooms, keep your bedrooms as bedrooms because they can boost your selling price. One of the developers I often stage for specializes in transforming warehouse space in Philadelphia. He says that he can add $100,000 to $200,000 to a property's price if he can divide the space to include an additional bedroom. I'm not suggesting that you add square footage or halve a perfectly good room to get an extra bedroom, but even a small room with a window, a door, and a closet will do. So, when you're deciding whether to stage a bedroom as something else (a workout or sewing room, for example), weigh the preferences of your likely buyers against the selling value of bedrooms.*

## CREATING VIGNETTES THAT CHARM YOUR BUYERS

When we stage homes, we often create stories about each space and build what we call vignettes about them (as we did in Figure 3–1, with the T'ang dynasty horse). Vignettes romanticize a home. Think about your prospective buyers and their generation. Create spaces that help these buyers dream about their life in your home. Whether you furnish a sun-filled baby's room, adorn the captain of industry's leather reading chair with the *Financial Times*, or stage a sparsely furnished, high-tech home office, you're creating snapshots that take your buyers somewhere appealing in the past, present, or future.

*Figure 5–3. Here is a great linens room on the third floor of a home we staged. Rather than forcing it into possible uses for today's living, we created a vignette based on its historic usage. The scene contains just enough for buyers to imagine how they might use this room, with its incredible light.*

*Figure 5–4. Okay, let's get real. Whose desk looks like this one? But it's appealingly simple, isn't it? Remember, you're giving buyers a vision of how their life could be if they buy your property.*

## AVOIDING MULTIPURPOSE ROOMS WHEN POSSIBLE

Ideally, each room should have only one use. If your home is small or if you have an open floor plan, you probably won't be able to achieve this goal, but it's worth striving for. Why? A multipurpose room suggests that you don't have enough space to devote a room to each purpose. For instance, a dining room that doubles as a home office says to buyers, "This home is too small for your basic eating and working needs, let alone your dreams." Take the laptop off the dining room table, remove the filing cabinet that's covered with a tablecloth in the corner, and so on.

Of course, in real life, most of us don't have huge homes, and we do need to use some rooms for more than one purpose. But the world you're creating when you stage your home isn't the real world; it's an ideal world where there's room for your buyers' needs and more. With that said, if you have no separate home office, by all means place a work desk in the living room. But set it up as a fantasy desk—tidy, carefully accessorized. This is the desk we all think we *should* have but usually don't.

Once you've reviewed the generational likes and dislikes in Chapter One, make a list of your rooms, if any, that need to be changed into other types of room to better suit your most likely buyers. Now you're ready to think about overall flow.

## Thinking About Flow

Buyers' eyes and feet must be able to move easily through your home. Each room must flow gracefully into the next in terms of usage, style, furniture arrangement, and color. Your rooms shouldn't be monotonously similar in style or color. Each room needs its own personality, but too radical a change from one room to another will be jarring to buyers. You need to arrange your home so that people are drawn into and can easily negotiate each room, and the view into the next room should be inviting.

Review Figures 2–11 and 2–12 in Chapter Two. The before photo is a good example of how furniture arrangement can prevent buyers from moving visually and physically into and through a space. The winterized porch is a strong selling point for this home, and the after photo shows how rearranging the furniture allows buyers to notice the porch and be drawn toward it.

One home we staged had a formal living room that felt like a department store display of inherited antiques. It was pristine and never used. The family spent all their time in a huge contemporary family room off the kitchen. I suspect that the formal part of the home could have burned down, and no one would have noticed until the next family holiday. Building a large contemporary addition onto a traditional house is not uncommon, but unfortunately it usually reduces the home's cohesiveness. I think of these big add-ons as the tail wagging the dog.

If your house has an addition like this, even though you can't change its size, you can alter the style and contents of the older and newer rooms so that they work better together. Furnish your contemporary addition with a few traditional pieces, and give the living room a shot in the arm with fresh pillows and contemporary lighting. Sometimes you just need to swap accessories, paintings, or pillows from one room to another. Repeating objects and colors from one room to another can also help your property flow better as a whole.

Note whether people can travel along obvious pathways as they enter each room, negotiate it, and exit it. These ideal pathways create the natural axes within each room. Is furniture blocking them in any way? If so, move things around and try to balance the furniture around these paths. It is amazing how many people place obstacles in the way of basic traffic flow.

As you stage each room, keep coming back to the question of flow. Are you arranging furniture so that buyers can easily move around in each room? Are you styling your rooms so that they're different enough to intrigue buyers without jarring them as they move from one to the next?

## Finding Each Room's Architectural Focus

In identifying your most likely buyers, you've already chosen your focus for the property as a whole: gearing as much in the home as possible toward the likely preferences and dreams of that generational group. Now that you've decided how your rooms will be used, it's time to choose the architectural focus within each room.

Your uncluttered rooms probably feel empty and airy, making it much easier to see them for what they are and to find their best features. If a room contains a fireplace, that's the feature you want buyers to focus on. People have a primeval desire to congregate around a fire. (Even if your fireplace is unattractive, minimize its shortcomings with fireplace tools, a screen, candles, and other accents.) Always lay the fire, ideally with birch wood. If you don't have a fireplace, perhaps the focus is a window; bay windows, arched windows, large windows, even a room's only window are all appealing. Pocket doors, a lovely view, hardwood floors, or even a room's proportions, paint color, or coziness can also be its focus.

> **What About the TVs?**
> *Remove TVs wherever possible. They become the immediate focus in a room. Even when not turned on, they are big black holes of ugliness. Additionally, any TV that's not a flat screen is dated and suggests that your entire home is dated. A TV is fine, however, in a room designated for media or entertainment.*

Walk into each room and decide what you want buyers to notice. Very often the feature is the space itself. After all, space is really what you're selling: the physical and emotional space for your buyers' needs and wishes.

If you have a yard or garden, choose a focal point or two outside (a flowering shrub, a terrace, a stone wall, a nice bench, something like that). Then sweep, arrange, paint, prune, mow, weed, mulch, or edge accordingly. Try to encourage prospective buyers' eyes to rove over to those points of interest.

## USING COLOR

First, a heads-up: Although this book contains no color photographs, if you wish to see any of the photos in this book in full color—and more color photos that don't appear here because they really make sense only in color—please visit my Web site at www.tailoredtransitions.com. There, you can also see colors that I like for each generation, updated as styles change.

Choosing a new color is a tremendously powerful and easy way to change the feel of a room and indeed of an entire home. A skillful change of color can make a dark room feel sunny, a cold space feel warmer, a small space appear larger, a grandly scaled room seem more intimate, and an oddly shaped room appear more properly proportioned. Conversely, badly selected color can make any space seem uncomfortable and unfriendly. The unsatisfactory use of color is one of the quickest ways to turn off potential buyers; fortunately, it's also one of the easiest to fix. Before getting into specific suggestions for using color, let's go over some basics.

### COMPLEMENTARY COLORS

Complementary colors fall exactly opposite each other on the color wheel (to see a color wheel, check out my Web site). Examples of complementary color pairs are red and green, yellow and purple, and blue and orange. We need to know this because complementary colors energize each other when they're in close proximity. They'll actually appear to vibrate. Occasionally you want this effect; usually it's too much. You're best off being aware of the phenomenon so that you can make it work for you. Diluting or graying down one of the colors in a complementary pair will reduce that energizing, sometimes overwhelming, effect.

### WARM VERSUS COOL COLORS

Some colors are considered cool (typically blues, greens, grays, purples, and silver), whereas other colors are considered warm (typically reds, yellows, oranges, golds, and browns). Even within specific colors, one hue can be warm (think of a piece of creamy, off-white stationery) relative to a cooler hue of the same color (think of a piece of inexpensive white printer paper). Warm colors advance, seeming closer than they are. Cool colors recede, seeming farther away. Light-colored objects appear larger and less weighty; dark objects appear smaller and heavier.

And why do you need to know these things? We all react to color, whether or not we're aware of doing so. If your buyers perceive your home as cool throughout, they may come away feeling a little distanced—put off somehow. If your home has a balance of warm and cool colors and you've used them in appropriate places, your buyers will come away more interested, more comfortable, more enchanted.

Imagine a kitchen painted a cold, slightly greenish yellow—how yellow would appear under a fluorescent light. Now imagine the same kitchen painted a warm yellow with the tiniest hint of orange in it. Which kitchen do you want to come downstairs to in the morning?

A word about lighting: Many of the new eco-friendly compact fluorescent lamps (CFLs) give off an extremely cold and unfriendly light compared to the incandescent light bulbs we're all used to. If you want to use CFLs, find bulbs with a color temperature of 2,500K or less, and *choose your paint colors under those lights.* If you can't find warm-looking CFLs, stick with incandescents unless you want buyers to leave your home feeling as if they just toured a hospital wing.

### MOODS ASSOCIATED WITH PARTICULAR COLORS

Although no color *always* produces the same emotional reaction in viewers, colors do have common cultural and emotional associations that can guide your choices as you stage your home. Here's what you should know about different colors:

❖ Red can be stimulating and provocative. It arouses sexuality and appetite, which is why so many tawdry undergarments and restaurant walls are red. In various hues, red can be a good choice in dining rooms, libraries, and formal bedrooms. Never use red with green: These opposites jar the eye and inevitably conjure up images of Santa and holly wreaths. Make sure any red you use doesn't clash with a room's wood tones or with any exposed brick.

❖ Orange can be intense, arousing, or—in paler forms such as peach or melon—relatively sophisticated. Avoid oranges that border on tan; these tend to come across as dime store nude stockings. Orange can add energy to a light neutral scheme, balance a too-blue scheme, and brighten a dark or cold room.

❖ Yellow can be cheerful or mellow, but avoid greenish yellow, which evokes bitterness, and avoid the jarring combination of yellow and its complement, purple. Yellow works well in kitchens, bathrooms, sunrooms, and children's rooms. It can add energy to a too-blue room. North-facing rooms always benefit from butter yellow walls.

❖ Green is associated with nature and conveys a feeling of refreshment and healing. Green works well with warm colors, but, again, don't combine it with red in staging. Olive and mint greens are hard to get right and therefore not a good choice in the staging market. Green is a strong color to use on walls and is best used as an accent color.

❖ Blue is the coolest of the cool palette but can also be warm. Like water, it soothes, replenishes, and tranquilizes. It inspires confidence. Navy blue has nautical and governmental connotations. Electric blue is dynamic and engaging. Periwinkles are playful and warm. Blue mixed with gray can be very cold but effective if combined with an equally strong warm color. Blue is a good choice in bedrooms and living rooms, and it makes an excellent accent color for almost any other hue.

❖ Purple is a complex color to use and tends to produce strong reactions ranging from "I love the lavender walls!" to "I really, *really* hate this purple room." You're better off avoiding it.

❖ Pink won't sell anything to men. Use it sparingly. If you have a girl's room, you may use pink accents, but dilute the sweetness of pink with white, blue, or green. Don't put pink on a wall if it's not already there—unless you're marketing to Boomers, who are more fond of pink than younger generations are.

❖ White can be innocent and timeless, with a feeling of simplicity. It can also be modern and sophisticated. Pure whites are stark in interiors unless relieved by a warming contrast. Off-whites, such as cream or vanilla, are warm and friendly. White is safe for large areas if offset with small areas of color. On walls, plain white is the color of rentals. To avoid this look, use tinted whites on the walls with bright white trim. White is the most effective when combined with textural variety. Use white the same way you'd use neutrals. For staging purposes, all bedding and towels should be white.

❖ Neutrals include beige, gray, taupe, and tinted whites. Classic yet contemporary, neutrals come across as enduring and timeless. They're at their best in combination with well chosen accent colors or as a way to offset works of art, dark walls of wood or stone, interesting architectural details, or dramatic views. In the absence of these things, though, neutrals can be boring and lacking in energy. Grays can be effective but are dangerous for staging because of their coldness and institutional connotations. Unless the gray is already there, don't add it.

❖ Brown triggers warm, rich, clubby feelings, which makes it a great choice for libraries and dens. Tans are homelike and enduring, whereas dark browns are masculine and strong. Avoid using browns in bathrooms or bedrooms, though.

❖ Black conveys power and mystery. It's a strong, classic, elegant color, particularly when combined with white. When staging, use black only as an accent color—*never* on walls—because it can easily become oppressive.

### COLOR AS A GENERATIONAL CUE

What do you think of when someone says, "Picture a 1940s kitchen"? Most likely, a certain color combination came to mind. Don't use color schemes from decades past when you're trying to sell your home because they'll make your home appear dated and remind buyers of their parents' or grandparents' homes. Here are some color schemes to avoid, because they still smack of their twentieth-century predecessors:

❖ White, olive green, and cherry red—the 1940s

❖ Peach, mauve, and chalky gray-green—the 1950s

❖ Psychedelic color mixes, black and white—the 1960s

❖ Harvest gold, autumn brown, and avocado green—the 1970s

❖ Denim blue, green, and white, or dusty rose and blue—the 1980s

❖ All whites and neutrals, monochromatic rooms—the 1990s

But what colors *should* you use in targeting a particular generation of buyers? As individuals, people have their own color preferences, and you can't predict those. You *can* find out which color schemes are currently the most familiar and acceptable to your likely buyers, though. How? Look at the interior design or home furnishing catalogs and magazines they tend to read and shop from. These arrive in the mail frequently, bombarding readers with the season's newest mainstream design trends. Essentially, these catalogs and magazines all say: "This [sofa, wall color, set of table linens, whatever] is all about you. This is how you want to live. And you're worth it. [And by the way, here are the colors that 'this' comes in.]" You can pick up a lot of ideas for using color and design, just by looking at what's being marketed to your likely buyers.

### GENERATIONAL PREFERENCES FOR COLORS AND DESIGN AESTHETICS

Here's where your most likely buyers are getting their own design ideas, along with some good color choices for each generation (all color names and numbers are Benjamin Moore paints):

**Boomers:**

❖ The stores or catalogs of Restoration Hardware, Bloomingdale's, Pottery Barn, Tiffany & Co., Neiman Marcus, and Mitchell Gold + Bob Williams; *House Beautiful; House and Garden.*

❖ Blue Angel (2058–70)—clear blue, not babyish; great for bedrooms or kitchens.

❖ Marlboro Blue (HC–153)—baronial blue; wonderful in living rooms, warmed up with reds and oranges.

❖ Moonlight (2020–60)—sunlit yellow-gold to brighten dark rooms.

❖ Pale Straw (2021–70)—warm cream, lighter than moonlight.

❖ Fairmont Green (HC–127)—good in libraries or bathrooms.

❖ Clearspring Green (HC–128).

❖ Southfield Green (HC–129).

❖ Red Parrot (1308) or Moroccan Red (1309)—for a bold library or powder room.

❖ Flush Pink (2081–70) and its stronger sister Pink Lace (2081–60)—only for Boomers; try these for girls' rooms, guest rooms, or bathrooms.

❖ Ivory White (925)—great for trim throughout the home.

❖ Use neutrals, but not browns, tans, or grays, in main living spaces.

**Jonesers:**

❖ Jonesers are the most daring generation colorwise: the stores or catalogs of Restoration Hardware, Anthropologie, Pottery Barn, Room and Board, ABC Carpet & Home, Crate & Barrel, and Calvin Klein.

❖ Coral Gables (2010–40)—bright orange with a touch of peach; chic for a bathroom or sunroom.

❖ Posy Pink (2080–60)—great for a small, daring guest room.

❖ Ocean Breeze (2058–60)—killer bright blue. I have it in my living room and it makes me very happy.

❖ Beacon Hill Damask (HC–2)—every color and no color. I love it.

❖ Weston Flax (HC–5)—like Beacon Hill Damask, a rich, wonderful, neutral tan.

❖ Saybrook Sage (HC–114)—useful taupe-y green, great with paintings.

❖ Woodland Hills Green (543)—strong, slightly olive green.

❖ Paradise Hills Green (550)—lovely spring green with no acid feeling.

❖ Autumn Cover (2170–30)—rich orange; goes well with many other colors.

❖ Suntan Yellow (2155–50)—just like its name.

❖ Semolina (2155–40)—stronger than Suntan Yellow; makes a real statement.

❖ Soft Chinchilla (2135–50)—wonderful gray that turns blue on the wall; terrific color for almost any room.

**Gen Xers:**

❖ Gen Xers are practical: the stores or catalogs of Crate & Barrel, Design Within Reach, Pottery Barn, Room & Board, and West Elm; *Metropolitan Home.*

❖ Soft Chinchilla (2135–50)—see under Jonesers.

❖ Saybrook Sage (HC–114)—see under Jonesers.

❖ Beacon Hill Damask (HC–2)—see under Jonesers.

❖ Weston Flax (HC–5)—see under Jonesers.

❖ Cabot Trail (998)—nice flat brown, goes well with white and blue.

❖ Bridgewater Tan (1096)—warmer than Cabot Trail.

❖ Berry Wine (2003–30)—red with a hint of pink; strong but great for bathrooms.

❖ San Francisco Bay (802)—a wonderful blue.

❖ Kokopelli Teal (648)—high-energy, southwestern flavor.

**Gen Yers:**

❖ Gen Yers' tastes are still evolving: for now, the stores or catalogs of CB2, Storehouse Furniture, IKEA, Design Within Reach, and West Elm; *Interior Design*. Try a hint of metallic color or mineral colors such as silver, gold, and bronze.

❖ Sherwood Tan (1054)—taupe with a hint of green; extremely popular in developers' condominiums.

❖ Yellow Finch (2024–40)—acid, zingy yellow green that sits boldly on flat neutrals.

❖ Forest Moss (2146–20)—olive green but definitely not drab.

❖ Riviera Azure (822)—soft blue with violet overtones.

❖ Mayonnaise (2152–70)—lovely, creamy, slightly yellow white.

❖ Philadelphia Cream (HC–30)—creamy tan; great on trim and ceilings to offset strong colors or on walls.

❖ Providence Olive (HC–98)—wonderful warm taupe; one of my favorites.

❖ Beacon Hill Damask (HC–2)—see under Jonesers.

❖ Blue Jean (2062–50)—very pretty blue; strong but comforting.

❖ Sweet Orange (2017–40)—nice bright orange; adds energy to any space.

### IDENTIFYING AND REMEDYING EACH ROOM'S HIERARCHY OF COLORS

Each room in your home should have:

❖ A dominant color that takes up at least 60 percent—nearly two-thirds—of the room.

❖ A secondary color, the next color that pops out at you as you stand in the doorway and squint.

❖ Possibly, but not necessarily, a tertiary color—the *next* color that jumps out.

Walk through your home and figure out the existing dominant, secondary, and tertiary (if any) colors in each room. Floors, ceilings, walls, and furniture are all part of this calculation. Count neutrals and whites as no color.

Unless they're neutral or white, your walls will probably be the dominant color. (If they are neutral or white, look elsewhere for the dominant color.) Your rug is probably the secondary color. Remember that wood is a color (brown, black, or tan); if you have enough visible wood in a room, that color counts as the dominant color and may need to be reduced or energized by other colors that you choose. (Cheap wood paneling on the walls is usually a '70s holdover and can easily overpower a room. Whitewashing it is an easy, inexpensive fix.) With neutral walls, even a sofa's intense color can be the dominant one.

If a room has no dominant color, you need to create one based on your prospective buyers' preferences. If a room's dominant and secondary colors are just all wrong for the generation you're targeting, or if they clash horribly with the colors in the rooms adjacent to them, you'll need to change them.

Balance a warm dominant color with a cool secondary color, and vice versa, to energize your home. If your colors are strong and your dominant and secondary color are complements, that's too much sizzle for one room. Calm the room down with a beige or tan. If your room lacks color and is a symphony of creams, add some color. The safest way to do this is to look at a color wheel (see my Web site) and choose a color located 45 to 80 degrees away from the color you're working with. Using its exact complement would be too jarring. If you have a green room that needs energizing, add orange pillows, not red ones. If your green room needs calming down, neutralize the green with a corollary blue or a neutral color.

Adding whites or creams to a colorful room allows the eye to rest. Bring in a large piece of white pottery, cream pillows, a neutral rug. Oriental and other richly colored rugs speak of age, and therefore dirt and grandparents' homes. You're better off removing any strongly colored rug unless it's brand-new and contemporary in style. Buyers would rather see a neutral rug, with color on the walls and in accent pieces.

A lot of people think that painting an accent wall is a great idea. It can be, but realize that the different color will draw attention and add visual weight to that wall. Too strong an accent wall upsets the balance in a room. If you want an accent wall, try using a color from the rug or going two shades darker than the dominant wall color. Don't add a new color to the room. One way to pull a room together is to paint the interior backs of built-in bookcases in the room's dominant color.

Counterbalance a weighty piece of furniture that's overwhelming more delicate furniture by painting the opposite wall with a fairly solid but not complementary color. If a long hallway seems endless, paint the end a solid color to balance the space.

*Figure 5–5. Even in black and white, you can see how a monochromatic bouquet can bring contrast, life, and elegance to a space.*

You can use fresh flowers as a color accent, but don't buy ready-made, multicolored bouquets. Ideally, create a bouquet that's all one color and all one type of flower—all daffodils, maybe, or all white lilies. If your region of the country is oppressively hot, consider adding white-blooming plants to your yard or garden to "cool" down the approach to your home.

Think again about flow as you choose colors for your rooms. A brightly colored kitchen attached to a mostly cream-colored rest of the home, for example, creates an imbalanced feeling. Different rooms shouldn't all be the same color, but the intensity of their dominant colors should be similar.

> ### Benjamin Moore's Aura Paint
> *If you're choosing a wall color, try Benjamin Moore's Aura Paint colors. Although they cost more per gallon than their counterparts, they're designed to be applied in one coat, making them ultimately less expensive. They all go with one another and include just a few hundred choices rather than a few thousand.*

## CREATING BALANCE

In a sense, we've already been discussing balance or the lack of it. Rooms that don't flow into each other smoothly or that don't allow for easy negotiating around furniture throw people off balance; creating a more consistent style from room to room or simply rearranging the furniture can correct the off-kilter feeling. Poor color choices can imbalance a room or an entire home; better choices can restore balance.

Why is establishing balance so important? In our fast-paced, global community, balance is the ultimate luxury. It is at the heart of the life we want to lead. Prospective buyers are probably selling their own home because of some imbalance in their lives. Maybe they're too far from their new job. Maybe their present home is too much work, too formal, too small, or too big after a divorce or after the children have grown. A home is a tool for achieving balance, and it is also a manifestation of the owner's balanced or unbalanced life. Remember that your prospective buyers are searching for balance, and style your home so that it offers a vision of a balanced life.

Studies show that human faces that are considered the most beautiful are also the most balanced and average. Unique and exotic faces miss the broader market. This is true in staging as well: You need to make your home average to make it appeal to the broader market of your prospective buy-ers—and that also means appealing to both genders, not just one. You may certainly give at least one room a distinctly feminine feel and one a classically masculine look, but overall your property should not feel particularly femi-nine or masculine. Now let's look at some more specific ways in which you should balance your home.

### AVOIDING HEAVILY IMBALANCED ROOM USAGE

A few years ago, my firm staged two similar, yet vastly different homes. Both were elegant, seven-bedroom stone houses built at the turn of the twentieth century. The owners of both houses had raised their children in them, and both couples had successful careers in Philadelphia. Although there was an extreme imbalance in how each couple used their home, that was where the likenesses ended. One house had no less than four offices; two bedrooms, the living room, and a library had been commandeered for office space for its two owners, one of whom worked every day out-side the home. To make matters worse, each room had a Jurassic com-puter connected by Ethernet wiring that ran through the house like a mammoth spiderweb.

The second house had no less than four living areas on the first floor, each with a bar and a large TV that dominated the décor. You could wander from room to room and, in any one of them, sink into a plaid-cushioned, cocktail- and screen-induced daze. Two of the rooms didn't even have names. The owners, when not working, lived in the kitchen and the bed-room, watching TV (yes, more TVs) and checking e-mail on their laptops.

The office-filled house was not comfortable, and the comfortable house was not designed to accommodate a work space. We transformed most of the work space in the office-filled house into a playroom and two bedrooms, because even though the owners' children were long grown, their most likely buyers would have small children. Using upholstered fur-niture, we further softened their library. In the comfortable house, we

*Figure 5–6. We infused energy into this colonial living room by adding contemporary and transitional furnishings that complement but do not match the rough-hewn beams and wide plank floors.*

removed several TVs, transformed one room into a library, another into a home office, and yet another into an entertainment center. The results: The formerly office-filled house sold to a couple with young children. They put in an offer after spending an hour in the playroom with their child, discussing the pros and cons of the property. The comfortable house suddenly felt so good to the sellers that they took it off the market, and instead sold the house that they had already bought to move into.

Take a few moments to review your choices for room usage and your prospective buyers' most likely needs in terms of rooms. Is your room usage balanced correctly to appeal to your targeted generation of buyers? If not, make the necessary adjustments.

### BALANCING THE STYLE THROUGHOUT YOUR HOME

Identify the style of your home, because its style will affect your buyers' perceptions of it. You need to know what you're working with. I often get asked, "Should I furnish my Victorian home with Victoriana?" or "Should I buy only high-tech furniture for my super modern apartment in the sky?" The answer is no, not if you're staging to sell. Remember, you want to appeal to your target market, and you're dramatically narrowing your target market if you stage in one specific style. Staging is not decorating, which bows to your personal taste. Staging is not historically accurate furnishing, which bows to the time period of the home itself. Staging bows only to the broadest target market possible. So figure out the style of your home, and then stage its exterior and interior in a balanced way that may soften the home's style in some ways and highlight it in other ways.

Styles vary in popularity over time. Except for a few staunch supporters (like me), the historic home is currently not very popular. Many people view historic homes as fussy, labor intensive, and intimidating. Their architectural details may be exquisite, but they may also represent a daunting workload to prospective buyers. On the other hand, if you've updated the systems and amenities in a historic home, then its historic features will add value. Mainly, you need to be aware of your home's overall style so that your interior and exterior staging balances that overall style by both complementing it and enhancing it.

### BALANCING THE FURNITURE WITHIN EACH ROOM

Take a squint at the room you're working on, and assess the balance of the furnishings with the room and with each other. Is there too much weight on one side because all the furniture is clustered there? Does one piece of furniture loom over the others? If a huge black leather sofa is flanked by two delicate cane chairs, this is not balance. This is a gorilla walking two greyhounds down the street. Remove the chairs and bring in something that balances the sofa's weightiness; better yet, ditch the sofa.

Even if the furniture has all the same visual weight, it it seems randomly scattered, this is not balance; this is aesthetic entropy. We call it the pincushion effect. Your buyers' eyes will jump around instead of flowing naturally toward the room's focus. Review "Finding Each Room's Architectural Focus" earlier in this chapter, if necessary, to find a focus for the room you're squinting at, then balance the furniture around that focal point. Remember also to balance furniture around the natural traffic pathways in the room. If

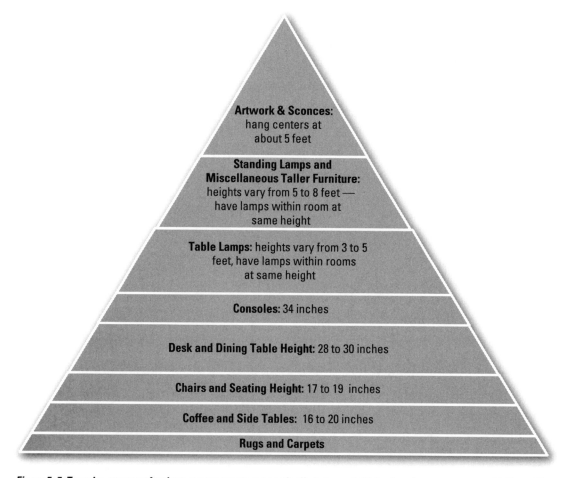

**Artwork & Sconces:** hang centers at about 5 feet

**Standing Lamps and Miscellaneous Taller Furniture:** heights vary from 5 to 8 feet — have lamps within room at same height

**Table Lamps:** heights vary from 3 to 5 feet, have lamps within rooms at same height

**Consoles:** 34 inches

**Desk and Dining Table Height:** 28 to 30 inches

**Chairs and Seating Height:** 17 to 19 inches

**Coffee and Side Tables:** 16 to 20 inches

**Rugs and Carpets**

*Figure 5–7. To make sure your furniture arrangements are vertically balanced, think of each room as a pyramid. Everything that is on the same level in the pyramid should be at the same height in the actual room.*

possible, arrange furniture symmetrically. If there's a chair on one side of a sofa, put a chair on the other side as well. Flank the fireplace with two chairs.

Ideally, don't place any furniture so that its backside faces a doorway. If your buyers can't easily enter a room, they won't sit, and, if they sit, they're more likely to buy. Think of your room as a stage set, and remove one side of your layout. This seems odd, but it works.

Balance in a room needs to be vertical as well. Think of the balance in each room as a pyramid. At the bottom is the flooring, then the rug (if any), then furniture, table lamps, standing lamps, mantelpieces, and art hanging on the walls. Like things should be the same height. Chair seats should be all the same height. Hang art so that the middle of every piece is at the same height. One common mistake we see is lamps at different heights in a room, especially mismatched lamps on either side of a bed or sofa. As etiquette is based on courtesy, staging is based on functionality. Anyone who has studied decorative arts knows the phrase "form follows function." When you're reading in bed, for example, you want your bedside lamp to function well for you; so choose bedside tables of the same height, about the height of the mattress top (for better function and visual balance), and choose matching lamps that are 24 to 30 inches high on the bedside tables, where they'll function best as reading lights. On either side of a sofa, find matching lamps that aren't too big or too small. Balancing tables and lamps this way makes a huge difference.

Sofas are often too big for the room. Their scale can dwarf what you're trying to sell: the space. Placing large sofas or sectionals in a small room is like docking an ocean liner in a small marina. To help you discern whether you're one of the many homeowners with Too Much Sofa, I've created an easy formula to use.

First, measure the length and width of a room. Then measure each sofa in the room individually; include any returns, that is, sections that make a right angle to the rest of the sofa. For staging purposes, the length of *all* the sofas added together should be no more than two-thirds the *length* of the

*Figure 5–8. The furniture arrangement in this living room allows for easy flow in and around the room (the hall entrance is to the right, just out of the picture) and uses repetition of form and vertical balancing to rest the eyes. The similar lamps reach the same height, the sofas match, and the two similar paintings are hung at the same level as the other painting.*

room, and the length of the *single longest* sofa in the room (including its return) should be no more than two-thirds the *width* of the room. For instance, if your room measures 12 × 15 feet, you can have 10 feet of sofa altogether (two-thirds of 15 feet), but no one sofa should measure more than 8 feet (two-thirds of 12 feet). So, you can have two sofas: either an 8-foot sofa plus a 4-foot sofa, or two 6-foot sofas. Given the choice, two 6-foot sofas present a more balanced appearance.

Successful staging comes down to the details. You know you need to consider flow, room usage, color, and balance in staging your home, but what about those details? You're not just choosing wall colors, you're choosing lamps, window treatments, things to hang on the walls (or to reconsider), and so on.

## Generational Do's and Don'ts for
## Lighting and Window Treatments

*Never forget whom you're trying to appeal to in staging your home. When you're deciding on lamps and window treatments to use, consider these generational preferences:*

**Baby Boomers:**

❖ *Do use Chinese export and brass lamps.*

❖ *Don't use chrome; Boomers think it looks cheap.*

❖ *Don't use a halogen desk lamp.*

❖ *Do use lined cloth curtains or just use valances alone to let in more light.*

❖ *Don't use wooden blinds.*

**Jonesers:**

❖ *Do use brightly colored ceramic or '50s retro lamps.*

❖ *Don't use brass lamps.*

❖ *Do use lined cloth curtains on chrome or painted or stained wooden rods.*

❖ *Don't use vertical blinds.*

**Gen Xers:**

❖ *Do use architecturally designed utility lamps (CB2 has these at good prices).*

❖ *Do use patterned shades and fabric pendants hanging from ceiling lamps.*

❖ *Do use contemporary swing-arm fixtures or pinhole ceiling fixtures for reading (only if you're doing electrical work anyway).*

❖ *Don't use table lamps.*

❖ *Do use sheers in acid colors.*

❖ *Don't use valances.*

*Gen Yers:*

❖ *Do use architecturally designed utility lamps (CB2 has these at good prices).*

❖ *Don't use brass lamps or traditional chandeliers.*

❖ *Do use bottom-up shades.*

❖ *Don't use vertical blinds.*

## CHOOSING ARTWORK TO SUIT YOUR BUYERS

Because small works of art, collections of smaller pieces, and montages all distract the eye and are hard for viewers to assimilate quickly, choose art from the largest pieces that you own. Large artwork creates continuity, which makes a room easier to understand. If you don't have any suitable large pieces and if you can't borrow, rent, or buy something affordable and visually appropriate (I'm not suggesting you buy or borrow an expensive original work for staging!), just leave the walls bare.

In hallways, hang art so that the middle of the picture is about 54 inches above the floor. Hallways are a great place to hang a series of art pieces, as are bathrooms; in fact, in staging these two locations are really the only suitable places for such collections. The presence of art can psychologically enlarge and cheer up hallways and bathrooms, which often need the help.

### Generational Do's and Don'ts for Choosing Artwork

*Baby Boomers:*

❖ *Do hang impressionist works, portraits, landscapes, nautical paintings, maps, or horticultural prints.*

❖ *Don't hang retro posters or abstract art.*

> ***Jonesers:***
>
> ❖ *Do hang strongly graphical work, black-and-white nature photography, expressionist works, or large color-field paintings.*
>
> ❖ *Don't display still life paintings.*
>
> ***Gen Xers:***
>
> ❖ *Do hang framed music posters; retro French, art deco, or other quirky advertising posters; abstract art; or photography.*
>
> ❖ *Don't use traditional landscapes or nautical paintings.*
>
> ***Gen Yers:***
>
> ❖ *Do display photography or abstract art.*
>
> ❖ *Don't display portraits.*

### USING MIRRORS TO ENHANCE SPACES

Mirrors are a wonderful way to transform a room. Hang them as you would an art piece, but make sure buyers can see their whole face in them. Like artwork, the bigger the better. They unify and enlarge a room, and they can greatly benefit hallways and oddly shaped rooms. When we're working in a twin home (meaning one half of a side-by-side duplex, a very common structure in Philadelphia), often we must place all the furniture against the outside walls to accommodate the home's hallways along its inner, shared wall. By hanging a mirror on inside walls, we can deemphasize the lopsided twin structure and bring in more light.

### BALANCING THE LIGHT AND DARK IN EACH ROOM

The contrast of light and dark makes life interesting visually. A monochromatic home with no color accents won't sell easily, nor will a home that's all pastel, all neon, all warm, or all cool. Some darkness makes a light space more intriguing, and the right amount of light can dramatize a darker space. Remember, you're the set designer.

*Figure 5–9. This fabulous living room already displays a lovely balance of furniture weight, space, and light versus dark. To fully remove the seller's personality from the room, I'd also take out all the collections and the Barbara Barry shelving at the far wall.*

## STAGING THE KEY ROOMS IN YOUR HOME

By the time you're ready to put your home up for sale, each room should serve the most sensible purpose possible, given your target market. Every room (and the outside area) should flow well, both within itself and into adjoining spaces. Each room should have a natural, visual focus with the furniture arrangement geared toward that focal point. The colors you've chosen should be balanced for warmth and coolness, and they should enhance the space you're selling by appealing to your most likely buyers. The contents of each room should present an idealized vision of what a wonderful, balanced, uncluttered life your prospective buyers could live in this home.

This section assumes that you've uncluttered and cleaned your home thoroughly (review Chapters Three and Four) and that you've followed the steps in this chapter so far. Now it's time for the finishing touches that are specific to different types of rooms.

### STYLING THE KITCHEN AND DINING ROOM TO SELL

A few years ago we were staging a home for a proper octogenarian couple who still did all their own gardening and cleaning in a 10,000-square-foot historic house. The property had an ancient but fabulous rambling kitchen with a staff sitting room and sunroom. In the middle of the kitchen was a retro linoleum table. When I suggested that perhaps we should move the mop, broom, and dustpan into a closet from their present location on the wall three feet from the kitchen table, I was asked, "Why in the world?" I explained that today's families pretty much live in the kitchen and might find it offensive to have a dirty mop so close to the eating table.

The owners were shocked. For them, even though they had no staff, the kitchen was the realm of the staff and should remain so. Even if doing so was inconvenient, the family should take trays to other rooms, even for breakfast, and leave the mop in its place. You need to think outside your generational box and gear your staging efforts to how your buyers will want to live.

In any age group, dining rooms are the least used room in the home, and they tend to feel stagnant as a result. Your goal in staging your home is to make all the space flow. Put away your silver and clear your sideboard. Try staging the dining room with less formal items, things that you might use if you actually ate in the room more often than four times a year. Consider hanging a contemporary painting (with an eye toward your target market's preferences, though).

Here are some general suggestions for staging the kitchen and dining room:

❖ Keep only three things at most on each counter in the kitchen (and see the advice for marketing to Gen X and Gen Y, in "Generational Do's and Don'ts for the Kitchen and Dining Room").

❖ Make sure the kitchen has a comfortable place to sit, so that buyers can envision their friends having a cup of coffee or cocktail while they cook.

❖ A large ceramic bowl filled with apples on the sideboard, or a flower or fruit arrangement in a bowl on the table, will help

*Figure 5–10. This stainless steel kitchen demonstrates balance and a feeling of well lit, clean, spacious storage. Severely limiting the number of items on the counter is appealing to younger generations. In fact, you should consider removing the canisters altogether if you're marketing to Gen X or Gen Y buyers.*

literally to bring the room alive. (Use real fruit and flowers, not artificial ones!) Another option is a large green plant in a ceramic planter in the corner (unless the green leaves clash with the wall color). Cover its dirt with mulch, river stone, moss, or some other decorative filler.

### Generational Do's and Don'ts for the Kitchen and Dining Room

*Never forget your target market! Here are some generational preferences to guide you in staging the kitchen and dining room.*

**Baby Boomers:**

❖ *Do have a comfortable place to sit.*

❖ *Do have canisters on the counter for flour, sugar, and so on.*

❖ *Don't have a kitchen designed for full-time dining.*

❖ *Do have a formal dining room complete with table, sideboard, and some visible china.*

**Jonesers:**

❖ *Do have a chrome, freestanding spice rack and French enameled cookware.*

❖ *Don't have linoleum flooring.*

❖ *Do have a formal dining area, if possible.*

**Gen Xers:**

❖ *Do have stainless steel appliances.*

❖ *Don't have anything on the kitchen counters, if possible. Keep the visible items minimal.*

❖ *Don't have a formal dining room.*

*Gen Yers:*

❖ *Do have a wine fridge.*

❖ *Don't have anything on the counters, if possible. Stay minimal.*

❖ *Do remember that formal dining areas are a low priority for this generation.*

### STYLING THE LIVING ROOM TO SELL

Living rooms should feel lived in and comfortable, yet they're often the most formal, dreary, unwelcoming room in the home. Follow these suggestions in staging your living room:

❖ Choose books carefully. In nonfiction, go for feel-good, hardcover books about style, nature, art, cooking, and lifestyle. Look for them near your bookstore's checkout line and in remainder bins, because they're largely unreadable. The fiction in your staged shelves should be novels that are both current and hardcover. Anything on the New York Times Notable Books list is probably fine. Best sellers are not always safe, in that some people—often those with the money to buy your home—disapprove of these so-called penny dreadfuls.

❖ Choose artwork that's two-dimensional, large, and visually arresting enough to draw your buyers' eye but not controversial, depressing, or personal in subject matter. (Any artwork that you could picture hanging in a dentist's office, however, has probably crossed the line between being not controversial and acting as visual novocaine. Don't use it.)

When you're replacing items in built-in, properly uncluttered bookcases, arrange books from tall to short starting at the outside edges of the shelves and moving inward. Put the largest books on the bottom shelf and the shortest on the top. You may place some books in short horizontal stacks for visual variety, but never on top of vertically shelved books! Only allow yourself three to five decorative items (depending on their size) per unit of bookshelves. They should all be the same color and style. For instance, do not have a ceramic kitten, a Chinese fan, and a pewter plate. Have three pewter plates or three Chinese fans. Pack the ceramic kitten.

---

### Generational Do's and Don'ts for the Living Room

*Keep these specific generational preferences in mind as you stage the living room.*

**Baby Boomers:**

❖ Do use chintz fabrics in oversized patterns with bold colors, and well maintained Oriental carpets.

❖ Do accessorize with silver, porcelain, and china.

❖ Don't use '50s retro furniture.

**Jonesers:**

❖ Do use expensive, neutral fabrics with lots of textures and spots of bright color.

❖ Do accessorize with colorful whimsical sculptures and adult games.

❖ Don't use chintz fabrics.

**Gen Xers:**

❖ Do use rich colors and textures (for example, layered velvets and chenilles).

❖ Don't use chintz fabrics.

**Gen Yers:**

❖ Do use humorous, ironic objects.

❖ Don't use wall-to-wall carpets. Use area rugs on concrete or plain flooring, or bare wood to create spare, dramatic spaces.

### STYLING BEDROOMS TO SELL

Bedrooms sell. Make the most of the ones in your home. Think about creating a bed-and-breakfast or nice-hotel look in the bedrooms. Here are some general tips for staging bedrooms:

❖ Cover all mattresses and box springs with mattress covers. Add a bed skirt unless a bed's legs are designed to show. All bed

*Figure 5–11. The hotel-like simplicity of this bedroom vignette makes any buyers feel they could sleep here.*

frames must be off the floor. Buy metal H-frames (about $50) and get those mattresses where they should be. Your room will seem bigger almost immediately.

❖ Iron the white sheets and pillow cases, and supply at least two pillows per bed head: two for twin beds and at least four for anything larger.

❖ If you can't get bedside tables of the same height, place books under one bedside lamp to make the lamps the same height.

❖ Get a headboard if you don't have one; upholstered, neutral ones are available online at affordable prices. They attach to H-frames and can transform a bedroom's appearance. If you truly can't get a headboard, add another pillow or two to each bed head.

❖ Provide a comfortable easy chair with a reading lamp to enhance the bedroom's appeal as a respite from the world.

You don't need to spend a lot of money to make a bed look inviting and even luxurious, as long as the sheets are crisp and white, the color of the quilt or spread works well with the other colors in the room (and is likely to appeal to your targeted buyers), and you follow the guidelines in "Generational Do's and Don'ts for Bedrooms."

### Generational Do's and Don'ts for Bedrooms
*Follow these generational tips to appeal specifically to your target market.*

**Baby Boomers:**
❖ Do add a chaise lounge, if possible.

❖ Do add matching Chinese export porcelain lamps.

❖ Don't add graphic throw pillows to the bed.

*Jonesers:*

❖ *Do add graphic throw pillows to bed.*

❖ *Do place a large, contemporary mirror over the bureau to open up the space.*

*Gen Xers:*

❖ *Do leave bedside tables completely clear.*

❖ *Don't have any action-filled pictures in the room. Keep artwork neutral and peaceful.*

*Gen Yers:*

❖ *Do simplify. Make the room as Zen as possible.*

❖ *Don't add any frills, chintz, or decoration. Less is more.*

### STYLING CHILDREN'S ROOMS TO SELL

Stage children's rooms so that buyers can imagine their own children in them. If you're marketing to Boomers, whose children are likely grown, style a child's bedroom as a nostalgic homage to an idealized childhood. Follow these suggestions to make a child's bedroom appealing to any buyers:

❖ Leave only clean, classic books, toys, and stuffed animals in young children's rooms. All the plastic stuff your children *really* love must go. Replace them with items like wooden blocks, Beatrice Potter books, Paddington Bear, a sailboat model, and so on.

❖ The bedding should also be all-cotton and white, not the 50/50 Spiderman sheets that your child prefers. Quilts and gingham checked comforters work well.

❖ In older children's rooms, which can present a staging nightmare, be sure you've prepacked all the clutter, unframed posters, outgrown toy and clothes, and so on. Remember: Bribery may be appropriate.

> ### *Generational Do's and Don'ts for Children's Rooms*
>
> *These tips will make children's rooms more appealing to your most likely buyers.*
>
> ***Baby Boomers:***
>
> ❖ *Do use blue and white, pink and white, checked gingham, or simple floral prints.*
>
> ❖ *Don't use bright colors. These rooms should be pastel.*
>
> ***Jonesers:***
>
> ❖ *Do have classic hardcover children's books.*
>
> ❖ *Don't have anything Disney or Pooh, unless they're pre-1970s.*
>
> ***Gen Xers:***
>
> ❖ *Do use bright, bold colors that will inspire confidence and incite Xers' children to great feats.*
>
> ❖ *Do lay out a creative wooden puzzle or two.*
>
> ❖ *Don't have anything too cute.*
>
> ***Gen Yers:***
>
> ❖ *Do stage a crib. Use neutrals, tans, and creams for the bedding.*
>
> ❖ *Don't have anything too cute or babyish. Not only is this cloying, but it's also scary to buyers who don't have children yet.*

### STYLING GUEST ROOMS TO SELL

As for any bedroom, stage your guest room as a sanctuary from the world. Keep it simple and inviting. Having a delightful space in which to host visiting friends and family is often a strong selling point. The following two tips will help guest rooms appeal to any buyers:

❖ Clean out the guest room closet completely to welcome potential guests (and buyers).

❖ If possible, remove the bureau and add a small, upholstered chair in the corner.

---

### Generational Do's and Don'ts for Guest Rooms

*Here are some ideas for making your most likely buyers feel drawn to your guest room:*

**Baby Boomers:**

❖ *Do place a water pitcher and glass on the bedside table, along with stationery on a small table if you have enough space.*

❖ *Don't have a platform bed.*

**Jonesers:**

❖ *Do include a soft, warm throw and a* New York Times *notable book in hardcover.*

❖ *Don't have twin beds.*

**Gen Xers:**

❖ *Do place a laptop on the bed, as if someone were about to return to it.*

❖ *Don't have a luggage rack.*

**Gen Yers:**

❖ *Do have a small flat screen TV.*

❖ *Don't keep books in the room. This is the Internet generation; sleeping with books around conjures up thoughts of allergies and dust mites for Gen Yers.*

---

## STYLING THE HOME OFFICE TO SELL

Most home offices are notoriously cluttered. I'm assuming that you've completed all the uncluttering steps suggested in Chapter Three and that your home office is already in great shape. Remember, a staged home office is a dream version of a work space. Prospective buyers don't want to see your bills any more than you do. Keep bills in that basket I mentioned in Chapter Three.

Here are some suggestions for setting up an idealized work space:

❖ Add one good-looking desk blotter with a matching pencil cup and paper holder (unless you're marketing to Gen Yers; see "Generational Do's and Don'ts for the Home Office").

❖ Replace any utilitarian desk lamps with a simple modern lamp. Look in a home store for the simplest large lamp, preferably in chrome (unless you're targeting Boomers, who dislike chrome). Avoid anything with a candelabra.

❖ Replace your office desk chair with a fun, modern side chair, or even an extra dining chair.

---

### Generational Do's and Don'ts for the Home Office

*Follow these additional suggestions to appeal to the generation you're targeting.*

**Baby Boomers:**

❖ *Do display leather desk accessories (home goods stores offer inexpensive options).*

❖ *Don't have books lined up on the desk between bookends.*

**Jonesers:**

❖ *Do include an overstuffed leather chair.*

❖ *Don't have visible wiring for the phone or computer.*

**Gen Xers:**

❖ *Do display one chrome canister filled with colored markers and another with colored pencils.*

❖ *Don't use leather desk accessories.*

**Gen Yers:**

❖ Do keep the desktop empty except for a black retro phone, a large white blank pad, and markers.

❖ Don't have any visible filing cabinets.

*Figure 5–12. Bathrooms don't need to be fancy, but they do need to be clear of all extraneous and too personal items.*

### STYLING BATHROOMS TO SELL

Bathrooms in a staged home are sanctuaries in their own way. They must not remind your buyers of you, personally, at all. Here are a couple of general tips for staging bathrooms:

❖ Put all medications and other personal items out of sight. If they stay in the bathroom, make sure they aren't in a drawer, cabinet, or container that buyers might justifiably open.

❖ Create a spa atmosphere as best you can.

Even if your bathroom is very modest, getting it completely clean and repairing anything that needs repair will already go a long way toward making it marketable; removing your personal effects is crucial, though. Don't leave anything of *yours* in sight that might derail buyers from fantasizing about the bathroom becoming *their* personal sanctuary.

---

### *Generational Do's and Don'ts for Bathrooms*

*Here are some specific pointers to help you create the bathroom of your prospective buyers' dreams.*

**Baby Boomers:**

❖ *Do use good porcelain canisters and soap dish; display Shalimar products.*

❖ *Don't use too much chrome.*

**Jonesers:**

❖ *Do have piles of folded white towels, and display Chanel products.*

❖ *Don't have tile that goes all the way to the ceiling. (I realize this isn't an easy fix.)*

**Gen Xers:**

❖ *Do have tile that goes up to the ceiling, and display Kiehl's products.*

❖ *Don't have linoleum flooring or gold fixtures.*

> **Gen Yers:**
>
> ❖ Do have lots of mirrors, and display Bliss products.
>
> ❖ Don't have pendant fixtures of any kind.

## GOING BACK OVER YOUR HOME AS A WHOLE

When you've finished staging all the parts of your property, take a walk through the rooms and around your yard, if you have one. Try to see your property with a buyer's eye. If you've successfully arranged your rooms to appeal to buyers rather than to yourself, you probably don't much like their new feeling of averageness and anonymity. That's fine, because you're trying to appeal to a broader, more generalized market, not to yourself.

Before I stage a client's house, I tell them, "I am going to try to please you in every way possible, except aesthetically." So be reassured that, if you don't particularly like the way your décor looks at this point, you've probably done a pretty good job. I hope you feel that your staged home isn't yours any more and that it belongs to someone else, someone with different taste, probably someone younger. As you walk through your home, see if anything jars you, catches your eye, worries you, or irritates you, and then try to remedy the problem. Review the earlier chapters in this book to make sure you haven't forgotten to do something important.

> **Have You Achieved Your Staging Goals?**
>
> Asking the following questions can help you confirm whether you've attained a feeling of balance throughout your home. If you own a house, count your yard as a room. As you look at each room, ask yourself:
>
> ❖ Is this room more or less equally filled with furnishings?
>
> ❖ Are all the rooms more or less the same style?
>
> ❖ Are the colors in each room about the same intensity?

❖ *Do warm and cool colors balance each other throughout the property?*

❖ *Are items on the same level of the room pyramid at the same height?*

❖ *Is the dominant object in this room counterbalanced in some way?*

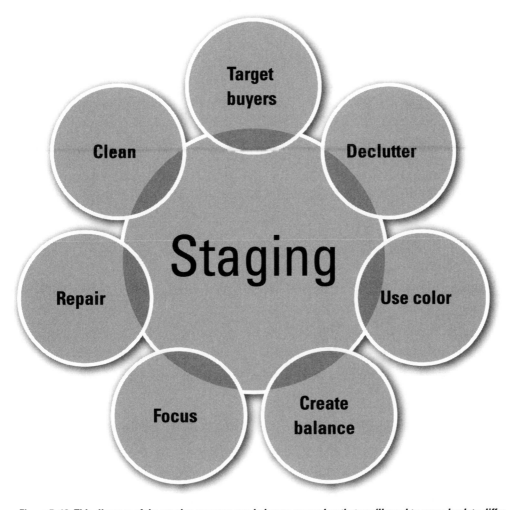

*Figure 5–13. This diagram of the staging process can help you remember that you'll need to come back to different aspects of staging as you go along. For example, you may realize, after rearranging the furniture, that you haven't uncluttered enough. Or your wall color may seem fine until you consider it against the colors in adjacent rooms and in terms of flow.*

## IF TIME AND MONEY ARE SHORT

Maybe you've just about run out of time or money by now. Your home is uncluttered, repaired, and cleaned, but you have to stage your rooms relatively quickly and cheaply. This can be done. You know your basic goal: making your home enticing to your prospective buyers, not to you. You've learned the basic elements that go into staging:

❖ Rooms that serve the right purpose.

❖ A sensible, natural way for buyers to move physically and visually throughout the home and within each space.

❖ Color used in ways that support your goal.

❖ A feeling of balance in every aspect of your home.

Just knowing these things will allow you to make the most of whatever money and time you have before your home goes on the market.

---

### *Must-Do List for Setting the Stage*

*Here are tips for a time-crunched, inexpensive staging sweep:*

❖ *In each room, remove three items that remind you of yourself.*

❖ *If and only if you've found three items to remove, add three items that you think your targeted buyers would find appealing.*

❖ *Count the number of cool-color versus warm-color rooms. If there's a huge imbalance, paint a room if you have the time and money. If you're out of time or money, add more cool accessories to balance the warm rooms, and vice versa.*

❖ *Squint at each room. Look at it through a camera lens. If anything stands out, remove it.*

## THE NEXT STEP: PRESENTING YOUR HOME TO BUYERS

By now, if you've faithfully followed the steps in this book, you've transformed your home. Congratulations. Don't underestimate the value you've added to your property. One couple whose home we staged was able to add $600,000 to their original asking price. Yes, $600,000. And they got their asking price after only two weeks on the market.

You're now ready to take the final step: presenting your staged home to buyers. In the next and final chapter, you'll learn how to get great photographs of your property. I'll also give you a sample timeline for the entire process if you have only a couple of weeks to get your home ready for the market. Finally, you'll learn how to keep your home looking great and ready to sell at a moment's notice. Remember, until you sell your property, you're living in limbo. The better you can present your home to prospective buyers, the more quickly it will sell, enabling you to move on to your own next step.

C H A P T E R

**6**

# Presenting Your Home to Buyers

*I dwell in Possibility . . .* —Emily Dickinson

**WHETHER OR NOT** you like the sparsely furnished, homogenized new look of your familiar old home, you may be finding that your staged home is surprisingly nice to spend time in. I've had several clients take their homes off the market after we staged them.

Balanced, uncluttered homes feel good, and your home will appeal to buyers much more now that you've worked to create balance and space in every room. In a balanced home, form follows function and the property supports the lifestyle and dreams of the owner, not the other way around.

This concept is not new; it's been around for about a century, since the end of the Victorian era, when Americans gained enough confidence to worry foremost about their own needs and only secondarily about their need to impress. However, the concept is rarely articulated, even though our domestic comfort is founded on it. "A good house," said a *House Beautiful* article in 1925, "is one that exactly fits the needs of the family for whom it

*Figure 6–1. A chair, a table, and light—those are the basic requirements for a reading corner. What staging does is to add the extras that draw in and delight prospective buyers: The chair is comfortable and attractive chair. The table is the right size for its purpose, and the light streams into the space in a lovely way.*

is built." *This is the big secret: Fit the needs and dreams of your potential buyers, and you will sell your property.*

## USING THE POWER OF THE CAMERA'S EYE

Of course, you can't sell your property if no one sees it or if your prospective buyers' first view of it is an unflattering photo that seems to highlight the armrest of your sofa. We discussed the importance of good Internet photos in Chapter Two (see "The First Look: Attracting Internet Shoppers"). Now it's time to go over the nuts and bolts of getting photographs that enhance the selling points of your home and make prospective buyers want to see it in person.

### TAKING ANOTHER WALK-THROUGH WITH A CAMERA

You've done this once, back in Chapter Three (see "Double-checking Your Uncluttering through a Camera Lens"), with the camera lens helping to pinpoint clutter, confusion, dirt, and necessary repairs as you finished uncluttering and prepared to repair and clean your home. Ideally, on this walk-through, your camera lens will reveal all your great staging work: a clean, uncluttered impression of your home's best features. If the lens captures something you don't want in your pictures, whether it's a personal item or a staged prop, remove it. Then get ready to point and shoot.

---

### *How to Take Your Own Winning Photographs*

*Even if you're not a professional photographer, you can greatly boost the quality of your photos by following these suggestions:*

❖ *Get a good camera. To begin, get yourself a good digital camera. If you don't own your own, borrow a good one from a friend. Remember that a significant portion of your buyers will see your home first in a photo on the Internet. That will be your one chance to lure them out of their chairs and over to your home.*

❖ *Use a wide-angle lens. Whether or not you have large rooms, try to get a camera with a wide-angle lens attachment. This feature will help you produce high-impact shots that show off the angles of a room and create a sense of space and proportion.*

❖ *Use lighting to your advantage. Keep the lights on in all the rooms you're photographing. Open the curtains or shades as well. Bring in professional photography lights, if possible; they flood a room with soft, diffuse light that bathes every corner, making rooms appear larger.*

❖ *Position yourself carefully before taking photos. In most cases, it's best to place yourself right where your buyers will be when they get their first view of a room. Try shooting the picture from different angles to see which gives the best impression of the space while making it look warm and inviting.*

❖ *Highlight your home's best features. Think of the features that make your home most appealing, both inside and out: things like a beautiful fireplace, the way the light comes in a certain window, a tiled roof, whatever they might be. Then make sure those features show up in your photographs. If you have enough space in your listing, add a few close-ups. Ask your realtor for advice on how or whether to print your images. The highest-quality printing option is best.*

### STAYING INVOLVED IF SOMEONE ELSE TAKES YOUR PHOTOS

If you're working with a realtor, someone other than you may take the photos of your home—which can be good or bad, depending on that person's level of experience. Your photographer may be anyone from your realtor to his or her assistant—or even a professional who hauls a 360-degree camera into your living room to create a virtual tour. (I prefer still photos; these tours are technically impressive, but they don't always flatter a room!)

Regardless of who's taking your photos, you should stay involved in the process. The designated photographer probably won't prepare your rooms;

chances are that he or she will just walk through snapping pictures. Don't take any chances. Accompany this person from room to room, asking how each one looks through the lens. Would the mudroom look better if that colorful scatter rug were removed? Would the dining room look better without that large vase of flowers on the table? Ideally, your questions will spur your photographer to work harder at setting up each shot, although, of course, they may also merely irritate him or her. Be diplomatic and emphasize that you really appreciate the extra time involved in getting the best possible photographs. Remember that even clearly professional and careful photographers are not considering your targeted buyers' preferences. No one cares about selling your home as much as you do.

If the photographer is clearly a novice, or comes through your home with a touch-screen cell phone (such as an iPhone or BlackBerry) or a disposable camera, you're not going to get good enough results no matter how earnest the effort. In that case, thank the person very much but insist on taking the photos yourself.

---

### If You'd Like More Personalized Help . . .

*If you still feel you need help staging your home even after following all my advice in this book, or if you are severely crunched for time and want a professional eye on your work, an e-staging service is available at my Web site (www.tailoredtransitions.com). Simply fill out a brief questionnaire and send me photos of your property; I will send you back a customized e-staging assessment within several days with easy-to-follow, inexpensive suggestions. My guess, though, is that you've done a great job on your home just by using this book and supplying your own hard work and creativity.*

---

## IF YOU HAVE JUST TWO WEEKS TO DO IT ALL

Obviously, I want every person who reads this book to follow as many of my suggestions as possible, including hiring someone to perform any major repairs rather than just getting estimates, taking the time to really think about the best use of color in your home, and so on. But sometimes life gets in the way of our plans. Maybe you've just found out, for whatever reason, that your home needs to go up for sale in *two short weeks from now* (or in some similarly alarming amount of time), and that's why you've bought this book.

Unless you're already living out of boxes or you have very few possessions, the prospect of having just two weeks to prepare your home for the market can be terrifying. The following step-by-step advice is designed primarily to get the "you" out of your home and get your property really clean, more than to help you stage each room. You don't have time for a full staging, and it's better to present prospective buyers with a clean, fairly empty home than a home that's still cluttered with your family's stuff. Buyers need to be able to imagine themselves living the life they want to lead in your home. Your job as a seller is to make enough room in your home for your buyers' needs and dreams by getting your own personality—and therefore many of your possessions—out.

Plan on a three- to four-hour block of time for most of the following ten steps, if you can. You're looking at thirty to forty hours of work right there. Steps Five and Seven, and possibly Step Six, will require more time to complete. Step Nine is short. So here goes—that was the starting gun. Follow these steps to boost your chances for a quick sale:

### Step One:
* Give everyone in your household a heads-up that the next two weeks (or however long you have) will be brutal, that you expect their full cooperation, and that you're willing to bribe them shamelessly. Note that "cooperation" can mean hands-on help or simply staying out of the way.

* Read every chapter in this book if you haven't already.

### Step Two:
* Find a realtor if you haven't already, and sign with that person (see "Asking the Pros: Interviewing Realtors" in Chapter One).

❖ Ask your realtor to schedule a preinspection with a licensed, highly reputable home inspector (see "Get a Preinspection" in Chapter Four).

❖ Ask your realtor for a good window cleaning service and make an appointment to have all your windows cleaned (see "Windows" in Chapter Four, under "Clean Is What Sells").

❖ Figure out where you'll store your packed boxes while your home is on the market, and make that phone call. Make sure the space will be dry.

❖ Figure out how you're going to transport boxes, rugs, and furniture to get them off your property. Rent or sign up a friend's truck as necessary.

**Step Three:**

❖ Say good-bye to your home as best you can, given your time crunch (see "Out with the "You": Disengaging from Your Home" in Chapter One). Addressing this need right now, even briefly, will help you complete the rest of the steps.

❖ Identify the group of buyers most likely to want your home (see "In with the New: Figuring Out Your Target Market" in Chapter One). Keep them firmly in mind as you prepare to put your home up for sale.

**Step Four:**

❖ Buy packing supplies and boxes (see "Everything You Need to Know about Boxes" in Chapter Three).

❖ Buy new house or apartment numbers to replace your existing ones if they're dated or damaged. Replace the numbers when you return home from your errands.

❖ Buy a large, plain, neutral-colored doormat to replace each existing mat. Toss the old ones and put out the new ones when you return home from your errands.

❖ Based on the results of your preinspection, schedule appointments with reputable vendors to get professional estimates on what repairing any major problems would cost.

**Step Five:**

❖ Spend twenty minutes in each room putting anything you want to give away into a pile in the middle of the floor. (Have a trash bag handy for things you are going to throw away.) Don't allow yourself to get bogged down or distracted. Your piles may include furniture, clothing, bedding, electronic equipment, paintings, books, extra pots and pans, the pasta maker you'll never use, knickknacks, gifts you've secretly always hated. This is your chance to give them all the boot.

❖ If you're not sure about an item, ask yourself if you really want to spend the time and money packing it carefully and paying to move it. If not, into the donation pile it goes.

❖ Throw the smaller things you've selected into boxes and bags. You can either put everything neatly by the curb—it may all disappear before trash day—or you can donate it all to a charity or a thrift store. Just get it out of your home quickly.

❖ Particularly if you have children or an "Adult Unclutter Dreader" in your family, Step Five is where the shameless bribery may come into play. See "If Uncluttering Seems Utterly Overwhelming" in Chapter Three.

**Step Six:**

❖ Pack up all photographs, mementos, and personal items that you can live without while your home is on the market (see "Out with the Personal and Possibly Contentious" in Chapter Three).

❖ In each room, pack two more boxes of belongings—clothes, books, utensils, and so on—that your family can do without until your home sells. Focus on removing items from built-in book-shelves and from closets or built-in drawers that buyers will be opening.

❖ Put the small, personal items that your family *will* need (such as medications) into closed containers out of sight, so that buyers won't see them.

**Step Seven:**

❖ Clean your home as thoroughly as possible (see "Clean Is What Sells" in Chapter Four). If you can afford it, hire a professional cleaning crew to scour your home from top to bottom. If not, consider bribing your tidiest friends with pizza to help you clean on a weekend day.

❖ Don't forget to clean your front door.

❖ Remake all beds with white sheets and pillowcases if you have them.

**Step Eight:**

❖ If you have a yard or garden, tidy them up: prune, weed, mulch, edge, and mow. Hire a yard crew to do all this, if you can afford to. If not, consider bribing yet more friends to help you (the ones with green thumbs this time).

❖ Make sure no shrubs are blocking your windows or paths (see "Pruning Your Shrubs into Elegance" in Chapter Two).

**Step Nine:**

❖ Notice anything that's blocking your windows from the inside, such as curtains or blinds, furniture that's too high, decorative items, and so on.

❖ Open the curtains or blinds, rearrange or remove the furniture, and pack up smaller objects.

**Step Ten:**

❖ Move all the boxes you've packed to the storage space you've reserved.

❖ If you have any extra time, review Chapter Six and spend the time staging your rooms as much as possible, geared toward your most likely buyers.

Ta-da! Your home is . . . not really staged, but it is definitely in good enough shape to show to prospective buyers. Any extra staging that you can do while your home is on the market will help.

## Keeping Your Home Presentable While You're Showing It

Every day that your home is actively listed on the market—whether you had weeks or months to stage it—you need to be prepared to show it. Follow these tips to ensure that prospective buyers will see your home in its best light:

❖ Sweep your entrance area every day.

❖ Pick up mail and newspapers daily and put them out of sight.

❖ Water your outdoor plants.

❖ Put fresh flowers in your front hall if possible.

❖ Keep fresh fruit in a large ceramic bowl, or orchids in a ceramic pot, on the dining and kitchen tables.

❖ Open all curtains and blinds.

❖ Pick up and hide all personal items.

❖ Make all beds, using white, crisp sheets and pillowcases.

❖ Wipe down all sinks.

*Figure 6–2. By now, you know this living room wouldn't appeal much to Boomers, but its contemporary look, with interesting graphic elements in the pillows and the poster, would appeal to many younger buyers.*

❖ Wipe down kitchen counters and around pets' sleeping and eating areas with Lysol.

❖ Hide all damp and dirty towels. Lay out clean, freshly folded white towels.

❖ Check all toilets for cleanliness. Keep the toilet lids down.

❖ Hide all evidence of pets as best you can. If you have pets that shed fur, you need to vacuum every night. Clean litter boxes every day. Empty the litter completely twice a week while your home is on the market.

❖ Leave your exterior lights on to make your home more visible.

❖ Leave interior lights on so that your realtor doesn't have to turn on overheads.

❖ Leave your home during showings. That means everyone in your family, including any pets.

That's it. You've done everything you can possibly do to help your most likely buyers fall in love with your home. In essence, if a home is carefully arranged with the owner's needs and wishes in mind, it becomes a tool that helps the owner live well. If you've followed the suggestions in this book, you've created a home full of generational cues that tell your targeted buyers that *this* home will not only meet their needs, but also allow them the space for their dreams and aspirations, so that they can live very well indeed.

I find that my staging clients are in limbo, living in a kind of real estate purgatory, until their property sells. Remember that no matter how well you've loved the home you're selling, your goal now is to live well in a new space. My goal in writing this book has been to get you to that new space faster and more efficiently—hopefully with more money in your pocket—

and enable you to create a new oasis for yourself. If my staging experience is anything to go by, your hard work will translate into a faster sale and a better sale price. Enjoy your clean, spacious home while it's on the market—and then move on to your wonderful new home.

# INDEX